Healing Ourselves, Healing the World:

A Manual of Mystic Meditation Practice
for Absolutely Everyone

Healing Ourselves, Healing the World:

A Manual of Mystic Meditation Practice
for Absolutely Everyone

Dr. Subagh Singh Khalsa

◎   ◎

Published in 2006 by
Simran & Seva Publishing
37 Root Avenue Chautauqua, NY 14722

ISBN 978-1-4303-0162-2

Cover and Book Design: Paula Carver
Printed in the United States of America

Dedicated with unending gratitude

To the spirit of Guru Ram Das:
Sixteenth century healer and saint and a constant guide in my life;

To Yogi Bhajan, my teacher in so many things; and,

To Subagh Kaur, my best friend, and my wife.

This molten transformation
We call life
Is ruled sometimes by joy
Sometimes by strife
But the whisper of love
Is waiting for your ears
And the spell of love is holy
Ever golden.

- Joel Simkin

Also by Subagh Khalsa

MEDITATION FOR ABSOLUTELY EVERYONE
THE SUCCESS OF THE SOUL
ANATOMY OF MIRACLES

Contents

Introduction

We are approaching a critical moment in human history. Our past has been filled with unending wars, greedy exploitation of limited resources, and an almost universal contempt for those who were different. Today we are plagued by the catastrophic consequences of our actions: continuing war, global warming, huge populations of displaced persons, massive starvation, thorough degradation of the natural world, wholesale extinctions of flora and fauna, ever widening gaps between rich and poor, and the loss of traditional cultures and their accumulated wisdom. What about our future? Will we turn the tide and heal the world or will we continue our downward trajectory until we are beyond hope?

In order to turn the tide millions of people have much to do on many fronts. This book is about one of those fronts, the most fundamental perhaps: healing the inner workings of our own consciousness and becoming a healing presence in the world. When, as individuals, we are plagued by fear, greed, pride, or anger, all of our relationships are polluted, all of our actions made less perfect. When we operate with awareness and compassion the effects are quite different. This you already know but what you might not understand is how much power you have to cultivate and practice elevated consciousness.

The world needs wise stewards of the environment and able leaders in business, government, and education. We need people of foresight and integrity at all levels of society. And we also need mystics, individuals who clearly see the oneness in all and infinity in every finite form. A hundred years ago there were only a handful of environmentalists; today there are millions. Fifty years ago virtually every corporation was driven by profit above all else; today there are exemplary corporations choosing sustainability over short-term gains. Today there are a few mystics with crystal clear consciousness and impeccable vision. We need to fully heal ourselves and thus take our rightful place among them. We need to create an army of mystics, committed to healing the world.

Here is where your power as an individual lies, whatever your vocation or avocation might be. You can realize a sort of perfection whoever and wherever you are and with that perfection uplift all you touch. We all have that power. Eventually, when there are enough such individuals, electronically and globally linked together as we now are, there will come a tipping point, a moment when the collective consciousness of humankind can begin to shift away from negativity and despair and towards harmony. This is perhaps the greatest project in history and you can be part of its success.

One doesn't set out to become a mystic. There is no course of study to follow and no well-charted path to mystic awareness. Nevertheless, it is my intention to show how everyday people, leading everyday lives, can have extraordinary meditative experience and bring that experience, that healing, into community life.

Meditation is not just for "stress management," although we certainly can use that. It's "spiritual," of course, but that word has been thoroughly debased and now means almost nothing. "Meditation," stripped of all its original intent, is used to quiet hyperactive third graders and end suburban karate classes. I've been to churches where the "pause for meditation" written into the service was observed with less than thirty seconds of awkward silence.

We should be able to do better than that, to go deeper. We have to. We need to approach our problems with fresh ideas, skillful diplomacy, and sensitive leadership but mostly we need wisdom. Some form of meditation, with its power intact, is found at the origin of all wisdom traditions. That's what those prophets were up to out there in the desert. My intention is to show how we can emulate their practices, transcend the limits of ego, and possibly know the unknowable. This is no small task for me or for you. I'll need to be clear about matters that are difficult to describe and you will need to sincerely and diligently practice in ways that are not always so easy.

In the mystical there is always paradox. We'll negotiate those contradictions, making some sense of the unreasonable, with language inadequate to describe experience beyond words. The mystical is, after all, mysterious. I've tried here to use language understandable and useful within any tradition, but language is, at best, a pale approximation of reality. However, this is a book about practice more than it is an attempt to describe the consequences of practice and with that I think I can be helpful, so here goes.

Let's start with a little story: something I experienced while kayaking off the coast of Maine. It makes a good metaphor.

The day had been especially fine, with effortless paddling and spectacular scenery. Although miles from shore, I felt completely at home. Rounding a big island and turning towards the mainland I felt a presence behind me. Looking back, I saw a fog bank so dense as to appear solid, coming on fast. When it caught me I'd be paddling blind. Somewhere along the coast ahead was a safe harbor at the mouth of a river but it was still miles off and I'd never find it in the fog. I landed on the island and by the time I did the visible world had been reduced to a few yards of beach.

The island proved fascinating. From the beach a broad path led into dense forest. Along it I found rock cairns, cleverly arranged. Further on, a granite farmhouse striped of its wooden parts was being restored and a massive new building I took to be an artist's studio was half built. Later explorations revealed beautiful hills, fields, forests, and beaches. I had plenty of food and water, a dry bed in the shelter of the half-built studio, and acres of island to explore, so I settled in to wait out the fog.

I waited for three days and nights. I meditated. I explored the island. I cooked and ate. I did some writing. Despite the diversions, I finally grew bored. There was a lot more to see further along the coast and I became impatient to be off.

In the fog navigation would be by chart and compass, by estimates of speed and position, and also by sound: the warning sound of surf against rock and the guidance of a foghorn at the river's mouth. Itching for a bit of adventure I launched the kayak and aimed towards a buoy the chart showed a mile north. Twenty minutes later it emerged from the fog, dead ahead. That gave me the confidence to keep going. A mile more and I glimpsed a second buoy a few yards to starboard. Further off and I would have missed it entirely and been unable to tell the magnitude or direction of my error. Little by little I made way toward shore. Eventually I heard the fog signal and a bit further on a squat lighthouse emerged from the fog at the entrance to the harbor. As I went up river, the sea fog cleared, almost as quickly as it had appeared, and I found myself once again in brilliant sunshine.

Those few days seem a fair metaphor for a life devoted to the "spiritual" (or "mystical" or whatever you want to call it). In our infancy, assuming we are well cared for, our consciousness is clear and bright, like a limitless ocean on a clear day. We experience pleasure and pain but essentially exist carefree, seeming to sense the perfection of our being and the universe we are a part of. As we grow older we find ourselves in a somewhat foggy place, fascinating and challenging to be sure, but somehow limited. We occupy ourselves with endless diversions, some of which seem quite important. We forget that our world is but a dream: a pale fraction of limitless reality. Few of us try to awaken from the dream and even fewer succeed. Awakening requires imagination, inspiration, skill, and persistent effort, much as I needed chart, compass, and hours of paddling to pass from fog into sunshine.

To reach the coast, I took a small risk on an unknown sea. I could have gotten lost or reached the coast at a rocky place with no chance of a safe landing, but without a little risk I was going nowhere. So it is with the mystic quest. We let go of the familiar and secure, leave behind old beliefs and addictions, set aside labels and judgments, and venture into unknown waters, using a whole new set of skills. Fortunately, the way has been made easier by those who have gone before, teachers who provide guidance where needed, like the buoys along a foggy coast.

With some effort I reached the greater freedom of the mainland but I had no power to lift the fog. That just happened. The weather was utterly beyond my control, and so it is in meditation. One may do all sorts of practices to release ego, let go of grasping and aversion, and find peace in the unending present; but no effort can dispel the fog itself. There is paradox in the mystic process: we exert ourselves to be more happy and free, but perfect freedom and happiness only appears in the absence of effort. It is just as well. Can you imagine how awful life would be if perfection were within our grasp, if only we'd try harder.

The metaphor would be perfect if I had gone on to develop further navigation skills and use them to help others find their way. It is my firm conviction that we are here to help one another, to bring a healing presence into the world. All of our practice inevitably leads in that direction.

The plan of this book is simple. We will give attention to eight fundamental elements of mystic consciousness. I call these elements (or states of consciousness) Stillness, Awareness, Courage, Compassion, Gratitude, Devotion, Surrender, and Merger, although they are often called by other names. For simplicity's sake each will be approached in a separate "lesson" in which you'll learn to cultivate the element within meditation and in everyday life. You will study some of the subtle structure of each element and practice techniques to awaken it. Bear in mind that this division into separate elements is artificial. The reality is that they are all always present in you, although they may be dormant.

There are other ways to awaken these inner states but meditation is the most accessible and the most reliable. What is offered here has been gleaned from thirty-five years of daily practice as a Sikh and a student of Kundalini Yoga as taught by Yogi Bhajan, but these elements are not unique to my tradition. They are universal and I address them in a way that should be understood by people of any background. You will find no difficulty absorbing these lessons into whatever practices are already familiar. At the same time I've avoided watering anything down. What I am sharing here is, I pray, the real thing.

You're not going to create these qualities of Awareness, Gratitude, Compassion, and so on but realize their presence within. These qualities are who you are, not who you need to become, and the process is a matter of remembering who you are, of recalling what may have been forgotten in the confusion of life. As you invoke these elements you may feel alive as never before. When all eight are fully operational the joy and liberation you experience will be magnificent.

Introduction

A fundamental premise is that happiness is our natural state, the state we were born into and the state we return to whenever our bodies and minds are in healthy balance. But what of the extreme times: can we expect to find enduring happiness in the face of natural or unnatural catastrophe? The answer is an unqualified "yes" and the secret to such happiness lies in the ability to awaken these qualities of Stillness, Awareness, Courage, and so on. This happiness isn't the glee of a child receiving a new toy, or of an investor reaping a huge profit. It is the mystic happiness of a wise elder, one who sees that external conditions are never powerful enough to sever one's connection to the Infinite, simply because that connection can't be broken, any more than one could separate wetness from water or gravity from earth.

As you go through these lessons be sure to pause often to practice the techniques. A pause sign (§§§§§) has been inserted wherever practice will be useful. In addition, at the end of each lesson, there is a box with instructions for one or two additional meditations that can increase your capacity to manifest that lesson's quality. It is my intention to remain available to help you with any difficulties you might encounter. For contact information and access to my earlier books and other aids to practice please see the Resources section at the end of this book.

This is not a work of philosophy. It's not even particularly inspirational. If you just want to think about mysticism or want something to help you feel good, this might not be the book for you. This is a handbook of practice, perhaps a difficult one because it asks a lot. If you prefer reading through quickly, plan to go back later to practice more, returning especially to the lessons you need most. What is given here is an outline for a lifetime of practice, with no end in sight.

STILLNESS:
The Bedrock of a Meditative Mind

"What is meditation? When you empty yourself and let the universe come into you."
- Yogi Bhajan

I couldn't guess how many people have told me they can't meditate. Somewhere they have heard that meditation is being awake yet having a completely blank mind, but nothing is further from the truth. Meditative stillness is not the absence of thought or physical movement: those are signs of coma. In meditation you cultivate a stillness that deepens your capacity to listen, to feel, and to taste life directly, unimpeded by mental chatter or physical agitation. This is not a way to deaden yourself; it's just the opposite: a way of being fully alive.

Begin by observing how your mind creates random thoughts, how it evaluates or judges, concentrates, drifts aimlessly, or gets caught up in emotions. Notice sensory perceptions, the ways your body/mind receives information. Notice your body. Where does it carry tension and where is it relaxed? Are there areas of chronic pain or others that feel real pleasure? Do you feel fully energized or some level of fatigue?

This is how we start, just noticing what's there. Our stillness is a dynamic state, one in which we can be aware but without adding unhelpful mental or physical reactions. It seems simple to be still, but you might find it difficult. Sit in an erect and comfortable posture (See box). Close your eyes and let go of shifting about looking for a better position. Don't bother to scratch every itch. Your habit is to create many thoughts but now create fewer thoughts. We're just beginning

Stillness

and you don't need to achieve anything. Just sit for ten minutes or more, with a little less thought, emotion, and movement than usual, as you are able. Don't struggle and don't judge yourself. This first practice is simply to discover a bit about what it is like to choose stillness.

———————————— §§§§§ ————————————

How to Sit for Meditation

Meditation posture is based on being erect and relaxed at the same time. Let the "sit bones" (the ischeal tuberosities) bear most of your weight. With your legs crossed, roll slowly back and forth on your buttocks until you dis-cover the position that puts most pressure on these bones. Put a cushion or folded blanket under them (but not under the thighs) to raise your buttocks to the height which lets your weight push down on the sit bones while at the same time you can elevate your chest and relax your shoul-ders. Draw in on your chin with-out tilting your head either up or down. Be "at attention" but with-out any strain.

If you need to, you can sit in a straight chair with your feet flat on the floor, spine straight, chin drawn in, chest elevated, and lower back neither swayed nor collapsed. Let the sit bones take most of your weight. Sit forward on the chair, not using the back for support. An added cushion can support your lower back, but avoid leaning against your upper back. Relax your shoulders and let your hands rest on your lap, with palms up.

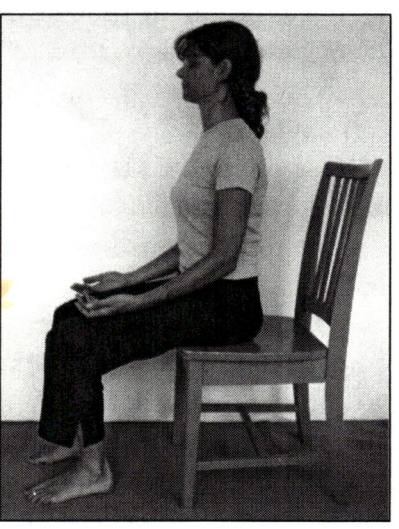

Comfortable posture is the foundation of meditation practice. Experiment until you find the right combination of chair or cush-ions so you can sit comfortably for a half-hour or more. ◎

With this first practice you have probably seen that stillness, this most fundamental element of mystical practice, is not so easy. To overcome obstacles to stillness most traditions have developed ways to quiet mind and body. I once visited the home of the Dalai Lama in India and watched in some awe as an aged nun did a long series of prostrations, alternating quickly and smoothly between full standing and full prone positions. Over and over she gracefully stretched out flat on the floor and then glided into a deep bow before raising straight up, palms together in salutation. A moment later she was again stretched out on the floor, which had been polished smooth by countless such devotions. She seemed to do this effortlessly, with a mind as still as her body was active. Her movements were a beautiful meditation-in-action but they were also preparation for deeper stillness.

I prepare for meditation with Kundalini Yoga (as taught by Yogi Bhajan) including posture and movement, breath control, eye focus, and mantras. It's all an end in itself but the yoga also prepares me to sit without disturbance and become more aware. All forms of yoga will help one's practice of meditation but Kundalini Yoga is especially powerful. It was originally practiced by warriors, peasants, merchants, and farmers; people who needed to fit these practices into lives that were just as busy as yours. It is quickly effective in awakening higher levels of consciousness.

Other paths use dancing or singing, drumming, stylized movements, prayer, rituals, or complex liturgy: all, like my yoga and the nun's prostrations, meditative in themselves but also preparation for something further.

One practice is to watch as breath comes and goes. Make no attempt to control breath, just mentally count "one" on the first inhale, "two" on the first exhale, "three" on the next inhale, and so on up to "ten." Then begin again with "one." Try this now, keeping up for eleven minutes or more. (Many of the techniques taught by Yogi Bhajan are practiced for eleven minutes. My experience has been that it often takes about ten minutes to really get "into" the practice with the last minute giving the greatest benefit.)

§§§§§

There are two ways to breathe. In thoracic breathing you expand the rib cage, puff out your chest and draw air in. This produces a relatively shallow breath ineffective for our purposes. In abdominal breathing, on the other hand, you inhale by letting the diaphragm drop. When it does, the volume of the thorax is increased and again, air is drawn in. This is the better way to breathe as it exchanges more air and is energizing and relaxing at the same time. Watch to see if your breath is abdominal, using the belly and diaphragm, or thoracic, using only the rib cage.

With an accumulation of mental or physical tension, the diaphragm tends to tighten and breath becomes more thoracic and shallow. Happily, you can release accumulated tension by reversing the process: choosing to breathe deeper and more abdominally. Put one hand on your belly. It should move out as you inhale and in as you exhale. Breathe slowly. Practice. It may take some time but you'll soon notice that deep abdominal breathing is both calming and energizing.

———————— §§§§§ ————————

After you are comfortable with abdominal breath you can begin to deepen your breath still further. Put your other hand on your chest and take a very deep breath, first expanding the belly and then the chest as well. As you exhale allow your chest to contract first, followed by your belly. Practice, gradually increasing the depth of your breathing, while also slowing it. You can breathe this way almost any time you're not exercising heavily. Try it when walking, talking with friends, preparing a meal, or watching a movie. Use it when under pressure. Especially use long, deep breathing as part of your meditation practice, relaxing with your breath prior to other techniques. Practice now, combining this basic breath control with the breath counting technique you practiced before.

———————— §§§§§ ————————

Stillness

The slower you breathe, the quieter your mind. Conversely, shallow, rapid breaths tend to agitate the mind. In your meditation now allow the inhale to take perhaps five seconds, then suspend breathing for five seconds, and finally allow five more seconds for the exhale. After a while stretch it out to ten seconds in, ten seconds with breathing suspended, and ten more seconds for the exhale. Don't "hold" the breath, just have a relaxed pause between inhale and exhale. Increase your times until you reach one minute for a complete breath (twenty seconds in, twenty suspended, and twenty out). This technique, taught by Yogi Bhajan, will take some practice but even in the earlier stages you will recognize the benefits.

Advanced Breathing Technique

Pull slightly at the "navel point" (three finger widths below the belly button) during the entire long, deep breath cycle. Maintain just a slight pull at the navel point, a gentle tension you can sustain for a long time. You'll feel the in-breath in the sides and back as much as in the belly. With a little practice this will produce a pleasant sense of energy being directed upward, flowing into the heart, throat, and head. As you exhale, continue to keep the pressure on the navel point and imagine the breath is leaving out the top of your head. Stretch taller. Begin working with this breath after you are quite comfortable with long, deep breathing. Use it at various times throughout your day, not just during yoga and meditation practice.

◎

As soon as you are comfortable with breath and posture, take your practice further, by using a mantra. A mantra is one or more sounds recited silently or chanted aloud. As I'm sure you've noticed, the mind generates an unending stream of thoughts. Fortunately, it only creates one thought at a time. A mantra is used as a single, well-chosen thought, intended to replace all the others.

Mantra practice is powerful. We all contain an egocentric little spirit that carries on at the slightest threat. If you are sick or worried or troubled in any way that ego-self immediately goes into its song and dance: "Watch out for that, this could get worse, be careful of what they think, hide those fears, put on a good face." You know the drill. When things are going well the same little demon also acts up. "Wow, this is great, make sure it doesn't stop, do whatever you have to do, but keep that good stuff coming." It's all very natural. We need at least some ego to take good care of ourselves; but we need to tone it way down if we want peace. That is a part of what mantras are for.

Some thoughts are positive, some negative, some confident, some afraid, some orderly, some random, some about the task at hand, others bearing no relation whatever. Such incoherent thought goes in different directions, making us less effective than we might otherwise be. Imagine you are preparing to meditate. As you sit you might think, "I am going to meditate for twenty minutes." In the next instant you think that twenty minutes is a long time, your knees might hurt, and you have other things to do today. You keep up nevertheless but soon a sound distracts you and you wonder what it might be and if you remembered to lock the door. You relax and breathe slowly and then realize you have been unconsciously rocking back and forth since you sat down. You stop rocking but a moment later find yourself thinking about a project at work. And so it goes. Your thoughts are incoherent, and nothing really happens.

Consider a different situation. You are an artist in your studio. As you paint the outside world seems to disappear. You see only the canvas and paints, notice no distractions, and continue work without interruptions. You become absorbed in the work and loose all sense of time. You feel no hunger, thirst, or fatigue. Your single thought is a vision of the work emerging before you. Hours later a prodigious amount of work has been done and a masterpiece is in the making. This is coherence: all thought and energy going in one direction.

Now imagine such focus and energy, such coherence, not directed at painting a picture, but on simply being still. Imagine filling your mind with a single thought that gently silences the little ego monster and any random thoughts that happen by. It's not an attempt to force out "bad thoughts;" it is a process of substituting something more useful. The practice is simple; you repeat a mantra consciously, in time with your breathing. With each inhale and/or exhale you say it aloud or silently, over and over, and allow it to replace other thoughts. Of course, you will not stop thought. Thought is a natural product of mind. Accept what thoughts do arise, but keep returning to the mantra. With this, as with all the practices in this book you will need to discover for yourself what the effects of the practice might be.

Select a mantra from those given in the box following or from some other source. Then sit in meditation with normal breath or long, deep breathing, fully conscious of each breath. After a while add in the mantra, coordinating its silent repetition to your pattern of breathing. You might, for example, fill your mind with the sound of "Ong," repeating it on each exhale. A longer mantra can be divided in two, using one half while inhaling and the other while exhaling. In Kundalini Yoga and Sikh Dharma, for example, it is common to inhale "Sat" and exhale "Naam." If you want to chant a mantra aloud (in which case it will only be on the exhale) pronounce it so you can feel the physical vibration of the sound in your throat, mouth, palate, and nasal passages. Let the tip of your tongue touch the back of your palate whenever the sound of the mantra will allow it, as on the "ng" in Ong or the "a" and "aa" in Sat Naam. Mantras are chanted aloud in many mystic traditions, and the effect can be powerful, especially in congregation with others. You may want to look in your own community for others who practice this way. We'll examine mantra practice further in the lesson on Devotion.

———————————————— §§§§§ ————————————————

┌─ **A** Short List of Mantras from Various Traditions ─┐

I am

Sat Naam (Gurumukhi: "God is Truth")

Wa-he Guru (Gurumukhi: "Indescribable Wisdom")

Ong (Gurumukhi: "Creator pervading all Creation")

Healthy am I; Happy am I; Holy am I

God and Me, Me and God, Are One

Empty mind, don't know

Ribbono Shel Olam (Hebrew: "Master of the Universe")

Zeh Dodi V'zeh Reyi (Hebrew: "This is my beloved and this is
   my friend")

Lord Jesus Christ, Son of God, Have Mercy on Me

Om or Aum (Sanskrit: "Underlying reality of all")

Svaha (Sanskrit: "Hail")

Allah Ahkba (Islam; "God is Great")

La Illa Ha Illa Allah Ho (Islam: "There is nothing but God")

Aum Maanpayme Hum (Buddhism: "Hail to the thought of one's
   own Enlightened Being")

◎

└──┘

Mantra practice is extremely effective, but your mind will still wander some. Whenever it does, the only reasonable response is to return to the mantra. The minds of great masters wander, at least occasionally, and the best they can do is begin again. The only difference between the student and the master is how often this happens; and it really doesn't matter. Both you and the greatest meditator of all time must begin again whenever the mind strays. There is no great trick to it. Just start again, grateful for your discipline rather than frustrated with imagined inadequacy. There is no perfection to be strived for.

Not following stray thoughts seems to reduce the tendency to create such thought in the first place. In the same way, not moving in response to every little discomfort seems to train one out of thinking such movement is necessary, so a little discipline will go a long way. This distraction will pass, conditions will change, and soon enough something else will come along to disturb you. Your job is to return to the mantra and allow all else to simply pass by. Later you will learn some other ways of processing the contents of your mind, but first learn to create stillness with simple breath and mantra practice.

Use a mantra within formal meditation and then begin to use it at other times as well. Repeat a mantra with each breath as you go about your day. Return to the practice whenever your mind has wandered or when you have been thrown off by a difficult event. These simple things will quiet and calm you. Now is a good time to pause again for practice.

Stillness in meditation can be further enhanced by simple techniques of eye focus. Within your field of vision are countless individual "events." At this moment you can see perhaps thousands of nameable things: a rock, a tree, a curtain rod, this book, letters and words on the page, your knee, and so on, and on. Each of these consists in turn of thousands of smaller, perhaps unnameable, events: the little substructures of everything you see. Each event has some effect, however small, on consciousness. Of course you don't notice all these effects but some do register and your mind may generate further thought and emotion about them, endlessly moving in response to visual input.

You can begin to deal with this by simply closing your eyes but even then thoughts will be triggered by visual memory and fantasy. To further reduce all the noise you can look at the "third eye." Close your eyes, gently cross them, and roll them back, as if you wanted to see the inside of the middle of your forehead. It is not a matter of seeing something there; this is just an eye posture that quiets the mind. In the beginning the small muscles that move your eyes may ache just a little, but this will quickly pass.

Related techniques include fixing your vision on a single point in front of you, looking a little cross-eyed at the tip of your nose, or gazing into the space a few feet away without focusing on anything at all.

In any case, the idea is to not concentrate on whatever you might see, but simply to keep your eyes still. Choose one of these and practice it along with breath and mantra. If it is starting to feel that you have too many things to do at once, just close your eyes for now and come back to specific eye technique later on.

Conscious breathing, eye focus, sitting correctly, and mantras are fundamental techniques for creating stillness and peace. You could set aside this book now and base your entire spiritual life on nothing more. Begin to practice sincerely, committing to a minimum of forty consecutive days of meditation. Even twenty minutes each day will create positive change.

Once you've begun your practice maintain awareness of breath, posture, and mantra while riding your bike, painting the house, or carrying out the trash. Take your practice with you to work. Turn off the car radio and the kitchen TV and chant a mantra while driving or cutting vegetables. Ultimately, build your life around ongoing practice, rather than practice being the uncommon time of stillness in the midst of a life of frenetic activity or emotional turmoil. Some of my most memorable non-sitting meditations have been on extended hikes and kayak trips when I made each day into one long chanting and breathing meditation.

I also vividly remember carving my first wooden sculpture when I was twelve years old. It was a small abstract piece in a bit of fine mahogany my father had brought home. One evening I worked on the sculpture with mallet and chisels and went on to refine the shape with rasps and files and finally with sandpaper, starting with coarse and progressing to finer and finer grits. The finer the tool the more deeply I became absorbed in the work. I continued without noticing the passage of time and lost any sense of separation among the tools, the wood, and me. I acted and the wood responded; the wood changed and in turn I responded to it. The emerging shape was a reflection of my being, and I, in turn, was reflecting and echoing the qualities of the developing sculpture. I had no thought of anything else.

Then, rather suddenly, it was done. The piece was complete and I was applying a wax finish to its gleaming surface. It wanted nothing more from me and I had nothing more to give to it. We separated then, the work and I, and I felt complete, not because the work was done but because in the midst of all the energy and activity, there had been a most profound stillness. I had worked through the entire night. Ten hours had passed without my noticing. All my energies had coherently gone in a single direction. With the morning light there came peace and deep happiness. Almost a half-century later this time "in flow" that I stumbled into by chance remains one of the defining moments of my life. You can intentionally generate such experience by bringing stillness and awareness to all sorts of activities.

In stillness something new, something transcendent, can happen. You may be surprised by what a quiet consciousness can produce. If you haven't already, it is definitely time to begin your practice. Begin with the techniques I've given here and also practice the "Meditation for Stillness" (See box, page 20). If you wish to lead a life of happiness and freedom from emotional upheaval the best thing you can do is daily practice. Practice every day, come what may. If possible practice with others, as the synergy of a group can be most helpful. Alone or with others, it is especially wonderful to practice in the early morning, before the sun rises. It is a quiet time, when it is easier to clear the mind and establish your connection with the Infinite. Get out of bed earlier than usual and give yourself the gift of practice. Even twenty minutes can clear away negative thought and connect you with the Infinite. You will benefit the rest of the day, so the earlier in the day you give yourself this gift, the more hours you have to enjoy the results. Over time increase the time devoted to practice. Two and a half hours of yoga and meditation is ideal.

A Model for Daily Practice

If at all possible practice in the early morning hours, before the sun rises. Begin by tuning in. In my tradition we start with the mantra "Ong Namo Guru Dev Namo," roughly translated: "I bow to the Creator in all creation, I bow to Its divine wisdom." We chant this aloud three times.

Whenever practicing the meditations given in this book (or any other techniques taught by Yogi Bhajan) be sure to begin with this mantra. Sit straight in "Prayer Pose," with palms pressed together and the thumbs against center of the sternum (breast bone). Inhale deeply though the nose. Chant the mantra on one breath. If you must, take a quick half inhale on the rest before "Guru." Repeat at least three times, using this tune:

Ong---   Na-mo---   Gu-ru Dev---   Namo---

By making such a declaration at the beginning of practice, you set aside, at least for a while, your individual ego, in deference to an unlimited identity.

After tuning in, engage in some physical practice: Kundalini or other yoga, Aikido drills, Tai Chi, or even simple stretches and calisthenics. Any of them will help energize the body and make subsequent sitting more comfortable. In whatever you do let there be quiet focus, awareness of breath, and the use of mantra, as these will elevate even a few sit ups into the beginnings of a spiritual practice. After these preparations, practice some form of meditation for a minimum of eleven minutes. Then, come out of the meditation but try to carry its spirit with you as you go about your day.

◎

Make a commitment to individual practice and to your group if you have one. Without commitment you might skip those days when you're not in the mood or feel so good that practice seems unnecessary, but these often turn out to be the most valuable times. Meditation practice only nourishes as long as it is maintained. Drop your practice and the hunger will return. Practice is the recipe and commitment the key ingredient that feeds the soul.

You'll face obstacles, of course, but most are merely logistic: Who will take care of the baby? Where will I practice? How do I wake up earlier? With a small amount of commitment you can easily take care of these matters. There may also be deeper obstacles arising out of addiction to old habits or fear of the new, so look closely to discover exactly what holds you back; then you will have a better idea what your commitment is up against, and where to put your healing attention. The following lessons with help with these things.

A Meditation for Further Stillness

Sit so you are comfortable, stable, and erect. Be still and begin to recognize the effects of gravity on your body. Notice the pull on arms and shoulders, pressure between your legs and the floor or chair, the weight of your inner organs. Feel gravity draw on every part of you at once. Feel how each tissue, every cell, is affected, and offer no resistance, except to maintain your erect posture. Let go of any tension. Continue for eleven minutes, constantly feeling gravity. Then, sit for as long as you wish, enjoying the stillness you have created.

This meditation is especially effective in tuning up and balancing the first chakra, the energy center at the base of the spine, the chakra most related to earthy qualities of stillness, support, and security: the bedrock of spiritual life.

◎

AWARENESS:
The Foundation of a Spiritual Life

"We make everything important in our life except learning about our Self."
   - Yogi Bhajan

If stillness is the bedrock of practice then awareness is the foundation built upon that bedrock. This lesson will dissect awareness, so its subtle structure becomes understandable. I especially want you to know the technology of awareness, how it is cultivated. Without the technology, exhortations to "be here now" would be nothing more than preaching. This lesson couldn't be simpler: all you need do is feel what you feel. But that doesn't mean it's easy. I've given a lot of instruction here and it might at first seem repetitive. However, each bit is showing a slightly different facet of true awareness and all are worth mastering.

Let's begin with more practice. Prepare yourself and then sit with eyes closed. Create a quiet inner space and notice the sensations in your body. There are gross sensations, immediately noticed, which reach out and grab your attention, and there are more subtle sensations as well. You can name the larger sensations ("pain in knee," "full belly," "tension in neck," and so on) but the more subtle sensations have no common name. These are the tingles and vibrations, the small currents of energy coursing through your body. Continually expand your awareness to notice and include more and more.

When you notice a thought, see if you can discern the actual physical sensations appearing along with the thought, but let them pass without reacting. This is most important. Every thought you have (as well as every event you perceive and every emotion you experience) creates sensations in your body, however subtle they may be. You've experienced what happens when there is an unexpected loud noise: you feel a shock in your body, even before your mind interprets the sound. It is the same with quieter sounds, with thoughts or emotions, and with any other event: they also create shocks of sensations, some dramatic, some barely noticed. Meditate now, noticing all the sensations in your body.

—————————— $$$$$ ——————————

This last meditation is just a beginning. To go further the challenge is to not concentrate on any one sensation regardless of how strong it is. If you're meditating and someone starts yelling in the next room, it's going to get your attention, at least for a moment. The challenge is to defocus your attention, to recognize sensations that arise in response to the yelling but to also feel all the other sensations of this moment, at the same time.

In this way, be aware of the sensations associated with any event. Remain still, conscious of the sensations, but never concentrating. Always you are feeling as much as possible, instead of feeling only the most intrusive sensations. Remember, it is the sensations, the internal experience, that is of value, not the event itself. (Why this is so will become clearer as we go on.)

This is the key to furthering meditation practice. You will have thoughts. You will have emotions. You will feel pain and you will experience pleasure. You will concentrate on some of these and sometimes your mind will wander. These are the givens. If you observe as all this passes by, you will find some measure of peace. But if you engage this reality more deeply, continually feeling the sensations of these things, in this particular un-concentrated way, something much more valuable can happen. That's what we'll explore in the lessons ahead. For now, set the book down and start to practice in this unfocused, highly aware way. Begin with eleven minutes or more.

§§§§§

Plan on doing a great deal of this practice, as it is all-important. Instead of just being still, you are choosing to be broadly aware within your stillness. Practice this awareness as a part of meditation and also bring it to everyday activities, making awareness an ever-increasing part of you. Go over this lesson several times to be sure you fully understand sensations as physical experiences within your body. They are not your emotional feelings. "I feel upset" is not a statement about sensation, but "tightness in my gut" is. Finding yourself angry, you might note "a shaky sensation in my chest, tension in my jaw and arms, an ache deep behind my right eye, and a strange tingling in my tongue." The challenge is to allow yourself to feel such things without concentrating on them and without concern for what they are called, what they derive from, what they might mean. An important challenge is to experience these sensations without wishing you were feeling something else.

"I'm tense because you made me angry again, and this just proves you don't love me" is not the statement of one who is simply aware, nor is, "I am trying to learn not to be angry." Just feel what you feel. This non-judgmental awareness is one of the most important skills you will ever learn, and is a most essential step in the creation of peace and happiness.

Distinguish between sensory experience (tastes, odors, sights, sounds, and touch) and sensations in reaction to these things. If you were to look up from this book and see your house on fire, there would obviously be sensations in your body in addition to the sights and sounds of the fire. If you were to look up and see the smiling face of a good friend, there would be other sensations, apart from the actual visual experience. As you sip a cool drink, there is the flavor and coolness in your mouth, but also other sensations, perhaps a relaxation in your shoulders or some subtle tremor of pleasure.

It's important to make such distinctions because these more subtle sensations control us if we're not aware of them. We can become addicted to or repelled by sensations, even if we don't notice them consciously. As we go through these lessons I will be giving some examples of how all of this applies in everyday life. These examples are taken from my own experience and the experiences of clients and students I've worked with. I've changed the names of these other people.

Emily's father sexually abused her when she was a young girl. He would lead her into his den and lock the door to hide his abuse from the rest of the family (although it is likely that Emily's mother was at least somewhat aware of what was going on). The abuse, which did not include intercourse, was just about the only attention Emily ever got from either of her parents and a part of her came to crave these sexually charged times. She came to me as an adult and, among other issues, we worked on her inability to be "present" during sex with her husband. Because they had children living at home, her husband would close and lock the bedroom door if he wanted to have sex. Whenever this "event" happened Emily felt various sensations in her body, sensations related to her appetite for attention and sensations of arousal.

Then there was always another event, entirely mental: Emily's fleeting memories of being with her father. These images would immediately conjure up still more sensations, ones associated with revulsion and shame. These were not thoughts ("It was wrong of me to have such a relation with my father") but unpleasant physical responses to a memory. It all happened so fast she was not consciously aware of any of it. To avoid her unpleasant sensations Emily would then mentally leave her body and proceed with sex in a removed way, literally watching herself and her husband from above. The only thing she was conscious of was arousal followed by unfeeling sex.

Without awareness Emily had responded to her sensations of revulsion and shame reflexively. She hadn't been consciously aware of them but nevertheless the unconscious desire to avoid those sensations had led her to cut off an important part of herself. Beginning a practice of meditation and pushing herself to be fully aware before, during, and after sex, Emily made great strides. She became more conscious of her actual experience and as she did her sensations lost their power. In the full light of day those sensations of revulsion and shame were simply discomforts, not fearsome demons. Like Emily, we have all cut ourselves off from some of our experience. Like her, we all need to feel what we've avoided, if we wish to heal ourselves.

Three important details of awareness practice need further emphasis. First, attend to everything, without discrimination. Normally we select out of the totality of experience whatever seems important: the particularly painful, pleasurable, dangerous, exciting, and so on. We filter out of consciousness sensations and experiences that are difficult to face or which seem to have no particular significance. Much of my counseling work is devoted to helping clients feel their discomfort. Be equally aware of all sensations, big or small, important or trivial, pleasant or obnoxious.

Second, don't focus. Normally we concentrate, however briefly, on one detail of experience at a time and experience life in a sequential way. First this happens, then that thing, then the next. In awareness practice we let it all in at once, becoming equally aware of all the sensations of this moment.

Third, judgmental thought about sensation generates emotion. Emotions then generate more thought and more emotion, and still more sensation. The emotions you create are based on subjective belief, prejudice, preferences, fears and desires, and so on but are rarely based on objective reality. If thoughts are negative, you create unnecessary suffering; if they are positive you might create attachment or a limited, circumstantial happiness; but in either case emotions block a full and straightforward experience of reality.

Reducing thought or emotion is almost impossible if you try to turn it off. Instead just feel the sensations that arise along with your thoughts and emotions. It is never a good strategy to push away part of experience; nor is it useful to indulge thought and emotion, following wherever they may lead. Simply feel what it is like to be you in the moment and include those sensations in a non-focused, non-judgmental awareness. It will require practice to do this automatically, so take some time with it. Whenever you notice judgment in yourself, pause to feel the sensations that arise in its wake.

Most of us are quite attached to our emotional patterns. We feel they are correct, even inevitable given our circumstances. Somehow we feel safe and comfortable within our little emotional boxes and it may take some courage to experience reality as it is, without defensive walls of emotion.

For a further exercise, sit now, with eyes closed. Become aware of the sensations in your body. As you do, let go of interpretation and naming of your experience and any thoughts or judgments about it. You might feel an intermittent coolness on your skin and tiny fluctuations of pressure against your body. This is what you feel. For our purposes you do not need to go on to name this experience "cool breeze" or think about how pleasant and desirable it is. Just know the actual experience of the event. Meditate in this way for eleven minutes or more.

Notice how some sensations appear quite strong while others seem weak. By not focusing on the strong ones you can become aware of more and more. Take your practice a step further and begin to "equalize" your awareness; giving the same level of awareness to every sensation. Give all your attention to each of the millions of sensations of each moment. This may seem a logical impossibility but it does hint at the experience of full awareness. It will take great inner steadiness. Be still now and practice again, allowing each of the sensations of this moment a full share of your sensitivity, regardless of how strong or weak the sensations may be. Develop skill at equalizing awareness.

As mentioned above, pure awareness also calls for not naming experience. It is not "breeze" or "sadness" or "sore throat" you feel but very complex collections of essentially unnameable sensations. Where there is no naming of an event, there can be a fresher experience of the event and of oneself in relation to the event. You may believe the "thrill" of a roller coaster ride is good but the "fear" of almost falling off a ladder is bad, even though the sensations of the two experiences may be almost identical. When thrills and fears are simply experienced as they are, without judging or even calling them by name, there is an opportunity to fully experience the richness of this; the actual, sensational experience of the moment.

Although awareness of actual experience is of immeasurable value, observation of experience has built in limitations. Some teachers don't understand this and encourage students to observe experience as one might observe a parade: a series of events passing by, observed from some small distance. Such an approach reinforces a sense of separation between self and experience: the exact opposite of wholeness and integration. Events become either "me" (the observer) or "something which happens to or around me" (the observed). As you practice, notice how you might see everything as if from a particular vantage point, located somewhere in your head. You might notice tension in your belly and subtly think of it as "down there" or think of yourself as "here" and another as "there." At first, the sensations of this, the way it actually feels to be an observer, might seem almost too subtle to recognize, but with a little practice you will begin to feel the difference between being separated in this way and being more fully immersed in experience.

A client told me about her son's emotional melt down on a pre-school class trip she had joined as an aid. Some small incident in the midst of all the excitement set him off. When her son started screaming and crying she was deeply embarrassed and did everything she could to get him to stop. In our session I guided her to relive the experience without trying to distance herself, feeling what she felt in the midst of it. She was able to feel her sensations, not as something separate she had to get away from, but as a painful but real part of who she was.

Then there was a shift. Without separation from her experience, and without her judgmental mind telling her the experience was embarrassing evidence of poor mothering, she felt a much simpler discomfort: sensations of tightening in her stomach, tension in her face and shoulders, and heat in her upper body. Despite the intensity of these sensations, they were tolerable and a lot easier to deal with than "I'm a lousy mother." Without harsh judgments, she didn't need to distance herself from the pain she felt and it turned out to be manageable, albeit unpleasant. With practice she found herself ever more relaxed in such situations, and better able to be a healing presence for her son, whose tendency to have such emotional outbursts decreased dramatically.

We refer to this immersion in experience, without separation or judgment, as the "neutral mind." In such a mind peace and happiness can be cultivated. Of course, it is easier when one is not in the midst of a stressful situation; and so we practice meditation in peaceful surroundings to develop skill at simple awareness and neutrality. In the meditation room we can more easily deal with small discomforts and imagined or remembered difficulties. Later, when there is a crisis out in the world, we are able to go through the harshness of it, without scrambling to separate from experience or make it different from what it actually is.

Now, meditate once again. You will need to be quite still. Then, notice how it is you might observe experience, from a detached point of view, and especially how it feels to have such a point of view. This is a subtle practice and it may take some time before the self at the center of experience is recognized. Notice how you tend to look at sensations, as if from some small distance, how the "I" seems to be getting reports from the rest of your body / mind, and how almost everything is about you: you in relation to others, you in relation to events, you in relation to your past and your future. There is a subtle way all this feels. Allow the sensations of it to happen, with full awareness, and gradually the sense of separateness will decrease. There may come a moment when you drop the sense of self entirely and know an especially clear consciousness. Practice often in this way until each bit of your body can experience itself. The central command post watching over everything, this phenomenon called "self," is superfluous.

§§§§§

The "self" is not substantial but is an ephemeral (and often obnoxious) phenomenon, expanded by fear and separation and reduced by awareness and love. It is possible to develop a more oceanic awareness beyond the limits imposed by self. Awareness practice leads to an egoless state outside of both time (the sense that events are occurring sequentially) and space (the sense that there is a distance between distinct objects). There is simply no way to describe such a consciousness but this ego-free zone has been called "the higher self," the Great Spirit," "God," "The Universal Mind," and a thousand other inadequate names. Experiment with this way of meditating to discover for yourself what it may reveal.

A final note: when one has created a state of neutral, ego-free awareness within oneself, one naturally becomes a healing presence, like a loving mother whose attention sets her child at ease. It is possible to intentionally cultivate this quality in yourself and develop it to a fine art. Your meditation practice can help to heal the world around you, much as it promotes healing within. As you practice awareness and stillness, everything about you begins to change. You become calmer, happier, and more able to deal with challenge. Your entire "presence" changes and you affect those around you in positive ways. We will return to the process of intentionally developing a healing presence in the lesson on compassion.

A Meditation to Increase Awareness

Awareness might be understood as how we promote flow: the unimpeded movement of experience through consciousness. Flow is associated with water and the second chakra (or energy center) located in the region of the genitals, bladder, kidneys, and uterus. When this chakra is in balance, awareness expands, unimpeded by either desire or fear. This meditation will help you achieve such balance. It was taught by Yogi Bhajan, who also taught the meditations at the end of the following lessons.

(continued)

Sit in a comfortable and erect posture. You will be moving your arms so if you use a chair choose one allowing the movements. Your upper arms are down with elbows at your sides. Your forearms are out in front. Position your hands so palms are open and thumbs point up. The palms face each other but not quite directly. Instead, rotate the wrists about thirty degrees so the palms face up just a bit.

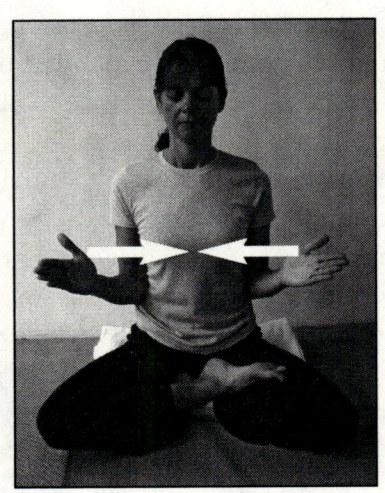

The action is a sharp, quick movement, something like a clap, but without the hands touching. Return to the original position and continue to repeat this motion rhythmically, about once every two seconds. Practice this meditation along with a recorded mantra, as it was originally taught by Yogi Bhajan (contact Ancient Healing Ways, listed in the resources section at the end of this book, and ask for "Ek Ong Kar, Sat Gur Prasad" as recorded by Nirinjan Kaur and Guru Prem Singh). As the hands come towards one another create a contraction of the muscles around the genitals. Avoid contracting other nearby muscles such as those around the navel and anus. Release the contraction as the hands come apart. It may take a little time to get used to this motion and unusual muscle contraction. Throughout the meditation focus your eyes at the tip of your nose.

Begin with eleven minutes and gradually work the time up to 31 minutes. To finish the meditation inhale and hold your breath while you tighten every muscle in your body. Hold for fifteen seconds and then relax. Repeat this twice more. Practicing this will make your quest for awareness more efficient. A powerful approach is to commit to doing this every day for forty days, come what may.

COURAGE:
Steadiness in the Face of Challenge

*"When you don't try to control everything, then you have
the freedom for relaxation and peaceful growth."*
- Yogi Bhajan

Once, I saw an elderly woman come out of her house with two Dobermans on short leashes. As she started down her steps a cat ran by and the dogs started after it, pulling the old woman off her feet and down the stairs. She lay bleeding from a deep cut on her knee, dazed, and afraid to let go of her dogs, who guarded her with a vengeance against the unseen assailant they imagined had knocked her down. The dogs' barks and growls got the whole neighborhood's attention but everyone just stared. I approached the woman, ignoring warnings from dogs, neighbors, and my own cowardly self. As it turned out, the ferocious dogs had a reasonable side, realized I was no threat, and all turned out well.

I relate this to help distinguish bravery from courage. Bravery, which is not so important to our discussion, is about disregarding physical danger in order to accomplish some important aim. That episode with the dogs was my little moment of bravery. Courage, as I will be using the word, is different. It is a willingness to feel sensations we find uncomfortable, to go to interior places we would prefer to avoid, of being present with the difficult. Sometimes such courage will lead to acts of bravery but here we will be more concerned with how courage leads to healing. In the previous lesson you began the practice of courage, as did my clients when they allowed themselves to feel previously unrecognized sensations. In this third lesson you will take the practice a good bit farther, using courage to heal painful emotions. (Although we won't emphasize it here the same approach is useful in coping with the pain of injury or illness. Such pain may or may not be eliminated through meditation but it can often be decreased, and always lived with more peacefully.)

Remember how emotions are created in the first place. An event happens, experienced as sensations in the body: the shock of harsh words, the shock when you hear of a friend's death, the very different "shock" of listening to beautiful music. Immediately, thoughts and judgments about the event and the accompanying sensations begin to form and an emotional response is created. This happens so quickly we tend not to notice the sensations, thoughts, and judgments sandwiched between event and emotion. We imagine the event causes the emotion: "What you said made me angry" or "I am saddened by Juan's death" or "I am thrilled because that music is so beautiful." But other responses in people with different personalities would have been just as possible. Emotions are idiosyncratic reactions borne of individual judgments that are, in turn, based on prior experience.

Thoughts, judgments, and emotions are themselves experienced as events, generating still more sensations, and more emotions, and so on. Without thought and judgment, there can't be emotions, either positive or negative, only experience itself: pure experience without attachment or avoidance, without fear or desire, and therefore, without the possibility of suffering. In thinking about experience, in judging it as either good or bad, and in reacting to our judgments, we create all our own emotions, pleasant as well as painful. Then we go on to validate our emotions ("I should feel this way") and give them power ("In order to regain balance I must express these emotions").

Courage is the ability to recognize difficult or unpleasant sensations and to remain present with them, without subsequent judgment and emotion and all the drama that can follow. It takes courage to be present because we find it easier to distract ourselves or to hide behind our emotions, using them to avoid whatever we are afraid of. Just as one who exhibits bravery on a battlefield is a warrior; one who exhibits courage in everyday life is a spiritual warrior. This warrior is fully aware of the difficult and intimately knows the sensations of it but does what is required nevertheless.

Healing and victory come from facing fears, desires, and other inner demons while maintaining full awareness and inner balance. A businesswoman can be a warrior, working to increase profit while remaining true to ethical standards. An old man with a serious illness can be a warrior, remaining peaceful despite physical pain and impending death. A student with challenging courses can be a warrior, striving for excellence despite myriad diversions. One can be a warrior while facing the everyday pain of another's criticism, the extraordinary pain of serious injury, or the gripping agony of a loved one's death.

Sit now in meditation, first becoming still and aware. After a while, bring to mind something uncomfortable for you, something painful in recent experience. The tendency with unpleasant sensations, of course, is to do something, anything, to distance oneself from them. You might squirm or scratch, come out of the meditation to see what the cat is up to, leave off meditating to reach for your addictive substance, or indulge in your addictive emotions. Now go in the opposite direction. Begin by recognizing your discomfort, feeling what you don't want to feel, and noticing ways you might be tempted to avoid. This is the crucial first step.

We feel what we feel because real events stimulate real sensations. We can no more stop sensation than we can stop the wind chilling us on a winter day. In attempting not to feel we apply protective layers between ourselves and the sensations and events which stimulate them, much as we might bundle up against the cold. But the events and sensations are still there, even if we hide behind dysfunctional layers of denial, distraction, or emotion.

It is as if you were living in a home with many rooms. Some rooms are quite comfortable for you but in others you've locked away your emotional demons, fearing they could wreck havoc if let out. You consume time and energy avoiding those rooms and keeping the beasts locked up and have that much less attention available for the rest of life. If, heaven forbid, a friend or relative visited or, even worse, moved in, the strain would multiply as you tried to keep your demons hidden. Sooner or later they'd escape their locked rooms, appearing in a flood of emotion. The newcomer might flee or team up with you in a dysfunctional relationship to hide the monsters from others or be forever resentful you hadn't revealed your secrets before she moved in.

A better choice is to courageously acknowledge the presence of the beasts; giving attention to the sensations they create right along with whatever else you might feel. Such awareness always leads towards healing and the disappearance of the demons. You may not know ahead of time what form the healing will take or where it will lead but be assured that courage is always a wise choice.

This is the warrior's choice. In this practice, you'll allow all sensations, but consciously choose to focus on the most difficult ones. This is intentionally un-equalized and concentrated awareness to face suffering and the demons behind it head on, entering the secret rooms of consciousness where they've been hidden. The theory is simple: the greatest suffering occurs where there is the greatest fear. Allowing the sensations of such suffering in full consciousness reduces your fear and its ability to control you.

Alvin's story provides a good example of the method. Alvin is quite intelligent, and a talented chef, but has difficulty focusing and has been diagnosed with Attention Deficit Hyperactivity Disorder (ADHD). In the chaotic kitchens of busy restaurants, he finds it a struggle to keep everything under control and often forgets important details. When he makes a mistake, owners, patrons, and waiters can become upset with him and Alvin's reaction had often been a rush of anger at the complainer. He came to me after losing one more job following another angry blow up.

I asked Alvin to put himself back into the situation at the restaurant, to mentally reconstruct the whole scene and relive the moment he first felt anger. This was not difficult. Next, I had him stay with his anger, to feel it in his body, notice the accompanying thoughts, and recognize how familiar it all was. This also was not hard as it was very familiar indeed. But something deeper was needed, something beyond "getting in touch" with the anger.

Alvin's inner process had been: "This experience is too painful and what brought it on is wrong and I must avoid it immediately." He would distance himself from the reprimand and his resultant pain with a display of anger. These displays were not unlike the feints and charges of an animal protecting its territory: a primitive attempt to scare off the intruder and restore preferred conditions. For bulls and gorillas, operating from instinct, this works well but for humans, operating from emotion, there is a high price to pay. Anger feels terrible, and it leads to consequences often worse then the events and sensations triggering anger in the first place. The same can be said of other negative emotions, the various incarnations of lust, greed, pride, and attachment.

If we had just stayed with the sensations of anger Alvin would have seen how miserable it made him feel. He might have learned to channel his anger and do less harm to his career, but he would still be angry. So I asked him to be still, to enter into meditation, and to look very closely at what happened in the instant just before his anger, even before he had formed thoughts about the reprimand. This is always an important step in the practice of courage. In the brief space between events and the emotions that follow, you will find thoughts about the events and, before those thoughts, the shock of sensations triggered by the event itself.

Alvin looked into the very small interval between the criticism he received and the anger he created and discovered there a deep sadness and a profound and complex set of sensations he simply called "crushed." These sensations whipped through him the instant he was reprimanded. They were part of the "shock" of the event. He had been unable to focus and had made another mistake. It was like it had always been for him, as long as he could remember. He was sad and angry with himself but even before he thought or felt any of this he felt "crushed." His associated thoughts were of not being good enough: no matter how hard he tried he would always mess up, always have people mad at him, especially those in a position of authority. These were his thoughts but they had been preceded by those awful sensations of being crushed. That is where we needed to focus if Alvin was to heal.

These sensations were very painful, certainly nothing Alvin would normally chose to feel, but as he courageously felt the intense pain of it, something shifted and a small miracle of healing occurred. Alvin experienced the pain, not as a horror that simply had to be avoided, but as sensation: mere sensation that he was, in fact, quite able to tolerate. Uncomfortable though his pain was, and perhaps for the first time in his life, Alvin allowed it to happen and stayed present with the sensations.

In a minute or so, he began to relax. The pain was tolerable so he could reduce his resistance. When resistance decreased, pain decreased, tension decreased, and resistance decreased still further. This cycle of healing continued and in a few more minutes Alvin was quite relaxed, sitting still with his eyes closed, aware of his own body in a whole new way, and not looking at all like someone with ADHD. Without defenses against his own sensations, he was free to know them, and a good deal more. For the first time in many years Alvin knew the pleasure of being alive in a relaxed body.

It takes courage to heal. Alvin acted as a warrior in going through his anger and into those crushed feelings, behaving as if his difficult sensations were what he most wanted to feel. He faced them directly, without resistance, and they were quickly replaced by sensations of peace. The demon was engaged with full attention and then it simply disappeared. Alvin is not done with all of this. It still saddens him to know how much ADHD has affected his life, but without anger he can face his sadness and has learned to use it to a higher purpose. He feels the sensations of sadness, allows them, and equalizes his awareness. Awareness of his sadness is used for his benefit. It takes him into a quiet meditation and he is blessed with peace. Interestingly, in those moments there is no trace of attention deficit or hyperactivity. Alvin feels pleased with himself and for the first time imagines being in a committed relationship and starting his own restaurant business. The agent of all this healing has been his courage to be.

Now it's time for you to meditate. Take a moment to quiet mind and body and become more aware. When you are ready, call up something especially difficult from your own experience. Perhaps you've been hurt by a rejection or face a catastrophic illness, in yourself or in someone you love. Spend a few moments conjuring up the situation and the palpable pain you feel in relation to these "events." Recognize what is most uncomfortable for you, being sure to give attention to sensations and not to thoughts or emotions (although you might use thoughts or emotions to help conjure up the pain). You want to know the actual experience, not your ideas about it or reactions to it. Look into the tiny gap between the event and your very first thoughts or emotions just as Alvin did when he examined the gap between being reprimanded and the welling up of his anger.

Once you are fully aware of these least desirable sensations (which are likely to be intense) draw them into you and draw yourself into them. Let there be no separation between you, as an observer, and the experience you are having. Reduce distance between self and experience, making self and experience one, reducing the distance to zero. Get to know your demon in a most intimate way. I cannot emphasize enough how important this practice is, if you wish to heal. It couldn't be simpler although you may find it challenging.

It will help to work with what I call "warrior breath". When you are fully in touch with difficult sensations, slow down your breathing and deepen each breath, being sure to use proper technique. As you inhale, imagine drawing in these painful sensations. Draw in more and fill your whole being with whatever you have been shying away from, going against the tendency to avoid pain. As you slowly and completely exhale, relax and let go of resistance. Continue breathing in this way for at least three minutes, very actively taking in the discomfort on the inhale and releasing resistance on the exhale. It may be frightening at first, but don't worry; this is going to be very helpful.

---------------------------------- §§§§§ ----------------------------------

Now take another step. At this moment millions of people feel similar sensations around similar problems. Whatever you are experiencing within, you share with countless others. This pain and suffering are not yours alone. With each breath imagine you are taking on, not your private pain, but this pain in the world.

You're not doing this out of ego, showing how powerful you are, nor are you trying to save the world. You are simply releasing attachment to your own "special" suffering and, in your willingness to take on the pain of others, declaring and experiencing your courage. You are not a victim but a hero, not fearful but courageous. (Not insignificantly, you are also acknowledging kinship with all of humanity: an important step in breaking the grip of ego and entering into collective consciousness.) Whether you are dealing with insecurity, serious illness, or financial setback, the process is the same. This warrior-like stance is very powerful. Take some time now to practice in this way.

There is a further step you can take. After you have released resistance and are feeling more relaxed, project your new sense of comfort out to those others who suffer as you have. Normally we want to draw more pleasure to ourselves. Now, go directly against this tendency. With each exhale imagine sending out peace and comfort from yourself, giving it away. In your imagination, let your inhalations take on the pain of others and let your exhalations carry pleasure and tranquility to them. This is part of the way of the spiritual warrior. Reread all these instructions now and pause for another practice session that incorporates all these techniques of courage. Continue until there is a sense of completion before coming out of your meditation. Plan on revisiting this process often, with any issues you find challenging.

§§§§§

You need not sit in meditation to be a warrior. As you go about daily life return often to this consciousness, eagerly taking on the harshest sensations life might offer. As you gain skill and experience you'll discover that courage, like all elements of mystic consciousness, is always available, whether you are sitting in meditation or standing on a hot, crowded bus stuck in traffic. I think you will find yourself more resilient than you could have imagined.

You can also use courage to heal addiction or attachment to your desires. In the lesson on awareness you learned to be present with your own experience, either pleasant or painful, and you have seen how transformative such awareness can be. As a warrior you can recognize cravings that may distract you from awareness. Whether you reach for alcohol, drugs, sex, chocolate, or TV, your addictions stand in the way of healing. Even positive addictions such as aerobic exercise or pleasant hobbies can distract your attention from where it is needed most.

A Meditation for Courage

Courage is primarily a function of the third chakra, located in the region of the solar plexus. The third chakra is the seat of personal power, motivation, and will. Here is where your fiery nature resides: in the will to excel and get things done, to keep to your course, to move towards goals regardless of obstacles, and to face the difficult.

(continued)

This meditation, also taught by Yogi Bhajan, will enhance and balance the third chakra. You'll be using a chanted mantra. The sounds of it are "Humee Hum, Brahm Hum" which means, "We are we, we are God:" a declaration of our shared unlimited nature. The mantra is a super-affirmation and an expression of mystic awareness. It is available from Ancient Healing Ways as a recording by Nirinjan Kaur and Guru Prem Singh.

Sit in "prayer pose" with palms pressed together in front of you, thumbs just resting against your sternum. Focus your vision at the tip of your nose, eyes open and slightly crossed. This posture and eye focus will promote a quiet mind and body while helping you to be neutral and balanced.

Chant the mantra as four distinct words. The tip of your tongue should touch the palate as you say "Humee" and the first "Hum." With all four words press the hands together as you pull in on the navel point (located three finger widths below the belly button) and then release. This compression and release is like the beat of the heart. One repetition of the mantra, with the four pulsations of the hands and navel point, should take four or five seconds. It's not as complicated as it might seem and once you get into the rhythm of the meditation it will become quite simple.

Meditate for eleven minutes only. To end, inhale deeply and hold the breath, pulling in on the navel point and pressing the tip of the tongue against your palate. Hold the breath for fifteen seconds and release. Repeat twice more then relax in silent awareness for as long as you wish.

◎

HEALING:
Serving Others with Love and Compassion

"Life is a flow of love. Only your participation is requested."
- Yogi Bhajan

A few years ago I visited South Africa, to teach and do healing and counseling work, particularly with the HIV/AIDS community there. One day I visited a home for abandoned children where many were dying from complications of AIDS. In one room were a half dozen such children, little ones whose lives would be over almost before they began. A terrible smell of decaying flesh filled the cramped room, from sores that would never heal. The aide caring for these babies seemed almost as listless as her charges and the children were comforted only by their own moaning or fitful sleep. I was drawn to one particular child, a girl of about four, slumped half way over in a high chair, too weak to hold her head up. She was as small as an emaciated one year old and looked very, very sick. Every breath was an effort for her and she emitted a small, painful sound with each exhale.

I sat by this little one feeling horror and even revulsion. So much suffering had been squeezed into such a tiny human being. The smell in the room, the weakness of this child, the presence of death lurking so close, the utter helplessness of the entire situation; all of it stirred up a crushing feeling in my chest, and a sense of weakness throughout my body. I had to feel all of this, there was no way not to, and I wasn't interested in escape, either by leaving or by being tough. I touched her stick-like arm as gently as I could, but she pulled back, either in fear or pain, and her arm fell beneath the high chair's tray. I chose then to just sit with all this, practicing stillness, awareness, and courage. My thoughts and emotions were irrelevant and the intense sensations demanded my full attention. Waves of powerful sensation passed through me. It was easy, in a way, to be present with this experience because it was so clear there was nothing else to do.

After only a few minutes, I felt a shift. What had been intense became less so, what had felt hard had become soft. I opened my eyes and saw a corresponding shift in my small sister. She was making what appeared to be a Herculean effort. Slowly, painfully perhaps, she pulled her little arm back up onto the tray of the high chair. For half a minute she struggled. The dull gaze in her sad eyes never changed. When she was finally in position she reached out with one tiny, bony finger, and touched my arm. When she did she lifted her eyes towards mine and for no more than two or three seconds, she smiled the saddest, weakest, and most beautiful smile I have ever seen.

Compassion or love or healing (I will be using these words almost interchangeably) is not an attitude or a philosophy, but a practice. Normally we think of love as an extension of affection or attraction, but it's not. Affection or attraction are pleasant emotions, within the personal self, borne of positive judgments about our experience, and are quite different from the deep connection of true love.

We enjoy the company of friends because we have pleasant experiences with them. They make us laugh or listen well when we need to talk. They may be affectionate or give us needed support. We experience their behavior as pleasant sensations, have positive thoughts about our friends, and we say we "like" them. If they are particularly good friends we might say we "love" them; but we are really expressing an emotional attachment to them because they give us what we want. Sometimes, if we get so much from another that we feel an unaccustomed sense of completeness in relation to them, we may say we are "in love." There is nothing wrong with such relationships, but they do not exemplify what I am calling love.

What happens if such a friend begins to change, if he or she develops habits we don't approve of, seriously disagrees with our dearly held opinions, or criticizes us relentlessly? What if, like the little girl in Africa, they were to become so transformed by illness we found it distressing to be with them? In the face of these changes we might develop new emotions and not want to spend much time with our friend. In his or her presence we would feel uncomfortable sensations, things we would rather not feel. Our attraction might diminish or disappear altogether. Eventually the friendship could end. Such is the possibility with mere affection.

Love, on the other hand, is not conditional, and not based on the pleasure and satisfaction the personal self derives from the relationship. Love is the experience of being absolutely at peace within ourselves, regardless of the sensations we are experiencing, while in the presence of the other. As my teacher Yogi Bhajan used to say, "Love is the experience of selflessness within one's self."

Real love (or healing or compassion) is present only where there is neither fear nor desire. All you need do to practice healing is apply the lessons of stillness, awareness, and courage to what happens in you in relation to the other, without adding any thoughts, concepts, or judgments. Genuine love and compassion are not emotions, and are not subject to change with changes in mood and circumstances. They are, in a word, unconditional, and this lesson is devoted to how one can practice being unconditional.

Tune in now as you have done in the other lessons, taking time to quiet your mind and body, and become fully aware. Allow your sensations to happen, with each sensation getting full but unfocused attention. If you need to practice courage in order to be at peace, take the time to do so. When you are stable in your awareness, bring to mind someone you have recently had a difficult or negative reaction to: someone about whom you have felt some revulsion, anger, lust, jealousy, or any other challenging emotion. Recognize your sensations in response to this person.

As always, attend to those sensations that arose in the moments before your thinking mind created the difficult emotions. Feel those original sensations, as in the lessons on awareness and courage. This is the central part of the practice, so take your time. Be sure to work with those first sensations, and not subsequent thoughts and emotions. Anger is not a sensation, nor is the belief that someone is an awful person. Those are emotion and thought, created in order to avoid the uncomfortable sensations immediately preceding them.

Look deeply into the gap, which perhaps lasted only a few seconds, between the event and your subsequent thoughts or emotions. Relax into this brief but all-important interval, attentive and stable in your sensitivity. The sensations may intensify, change, or disappear entirely: these consequences of awareness are not under your control. The practice is simply to become comfortable with your discomfort, allowing it plenty of room, without attempting to change it. Know the discomfort in you but know thousands of other sensations as well. There is enough room for all of it.

If you are diligent in this practice you will become peaceful, even joyful, in the presence of the other. That was my experience with the little AIDS patient. Through no fault of her own she was very difficult to be with and it took a little courage to include her in my meditative space. Love doesn't mean your preferences will change or you will approve of behavior or conditions you haven't previously, but it does mean you won't need to protect yourself from feeling what you feel. The actual experience you are having, whether it is pleasant or unpleasant, becomes the doorway into a joyful meditation. Protective emotions are simply not needed.

If you have meditated in this way you can find peace within yourself even without a resolution of any problem between you and the other. This is essential. In my experience in Africa, none of the outer conditions changed but my little friend and I shared real love. Such love, of course, is what you really want; this connection is the true end of all your desires. When I guide clients into a meditation like this, starting with their most painful emotions, they are amazed to find the pathway from pain to joy so deliciously short and sweet. Using negative emotion as a doorway and stepping through it into a sensitive space is not at all difficult if you work with the sensations in your body instead of the thoughts and emotions in your mind. Sensations are easy to make peace with whereas negative emotions are not. Fearlessly feeling sensations will quickly take you to a deep, still, interior place where there is no suffering and no defense or protection needed. These are the conditions for love.

Now, for a gratifying surprise, try the identical practice starting with a pleasant experience you've had with someone you enjoy. Allow the sensations of your "positive" experience in the same way you just did with a "negative" experience. Don't think about the event or the person (any more than is necessary to conjure up the memory) or get lost in your emotions. Just feel the sensations as they are, right along with everything else happening right now. Soon, you'll again find yourself in a peaceful inner place, free of desire. You will be in "love," that condition of quiet bliss, beyond mere affection.

§§§§§

Continue to heal in this way over time. After a few sessions you'll be able to take this show on the road. In conversation with a friend you might notice a feeling of tightness in your throat if she says something challenging. Your thinking and emoting self might want to throw up a defense or you might be inclined to swallow your feelings, but now you have a healing alternative. Simply feel the tension and do nothing. Or, you might be with someone to whom you are inappropriately sexually attracted. Feel the sensations of your attraction, chose "nothought" and no action, and simply know yourself as the tension of desire moves on. You can practice in the same way in any encounter, no matter what. The very best healing is when your body or mind receives healing from you.

The love you are practicing is the basis of compassion and meditative healing. What is compassion, after all, if not the ability to be fully present with another (or with yourself), without regard to your own fears or desires? And, what is the effect of such a neutral presence, if

Healing

not greater peace and healing for all? When Mother Theresa first
encountered the poorest of the poor in India she might very well have
recoiled from much of what she felt; but she had the courage to stay
with her sensations and allow them to touch her, perhaps even in
places where she was exquisitely tender. As she did, she was transformed and became more and more able to be with those people intimately, free of fearful, self-centered reactions. She found her great compassion and love, not by suppressing inner horror, but by allowing it.
When she did, she became a truly healing presence and an inspiration
for millions.

There is a technique to this. I am not saying to you "be compassionate" I am saying, "practice compassion." By developing our presence in this way we can all be healers. When I meditated with the little South African girl I held in consciousness a simple intention for
healing: what might happen if all ego were removed. I didn't think
about healing, conceptualizing what it might look like in these extraordinary circumstances, or how much I desired it. I simply intended the
space we were entering together to be healing. I am not speaking of
cures using drugs or surgery or herbal remedies, or even psychic healing. The healing I intended was the healing of love, the ultimate elixir,
of being present without conditions, fears, or desires and I had no idea
at the outset what form that healing might take.

Some people think "spiritual" healing must be about energy and
make effort to send energy to the other, or fix them with some esoteric
technique or another. Others think they need to know more about the
other to diagnose or understand his or her difficulties. It is all well and
good if you want to do those things but for pure love and meditative
healing simply be present and hold an intention for healing.

To practice healing with others, have them relax with eyes closed.
Sit close by, tune in, and begin your meditation, becoming still and
aware in the usual way. When you feel stable, simply touch your friend
or client on the arm, indicating you are in a relationship of healing. The
touch is not a way to transfer energy, "read" the other, or send love. It
is just a simple acknowledgement of the relation and your intention for
the meditative space you share to be healing. Then continue in your
meditation, no more, no less.

◎ 46 ◎

You are not doing anything new, only including in your meditation this other person, just as you might include any event. Interesting sensations may or may not arise but you should not assume anything you experience has special meaning. Just meditate in a neutral way. After some time you may sense completion; if not, simply continue as long as you wish.

––––––––––––––––––––––– §§§§§ –––––––––––––––––––––––

A challenging part of this practice is to allow everything. If you are in a healing session and have had a stomachache for two days you might assume the ache is irrelevant and shouldn't be included. But to ignore that pain means that you cut off a part of yourself, that you are less whole: not a good way to help restore wholeness in another.

Another challenge is to not interpret your experience, especially in the beginning. Later you may get inklings of something that would be helpful, some advice or treatment you can give, but for now just allow whatever experience shows up. You may be surprised by how healing that is, for both of you.

Perhaps most challenging of all is to avoid thinking you are the healer. You are not. You are maintaining an awareness and a presence in which healing can happen. If you think the healing is because of you, you risk spiritual ego, a most hideous disease.

This healing is the simplest imaginable. There is no diagnosis, no remedy, no action, no mental, physical, or spiritual force applied, not even a specific result being sought. There is only your sensitive presence and an intention for healing; in a word, there is only love. After some practice you may modify the intent slightly, holding, for example, an intention to heal the immune system, or reduce anxiety; but keep it simple, especially in the beginning. The more specific you make your intention, the more likely you are to bring limiting ideas into the meditative space.

You need practice to understand how powerful this is but a few words about my experience may encourage you. Working with AIDS patients in Africa or with someone's sore back at home, I never claim to cure disease. However, meditative healing does reliably enhance the capacity for self-healing. Body and mind are remarkably effective self-healers, and this is a lot of what meditative healing is about. Often there appears to be a cure, someone coming with a problem and leaving without it, but it's always a matter of the innate capacity for healing getting the support it needs. Full attention was the missing ingredient. There is no great mystery in this. You already know how wonderful loving attention feels, and how deeply it can touch you.

In a different South African facility for mothers and children with AIDS, I saw enormous despair. Mothers were dying leaving their HIV infected babies in the care of other mothers, already too sick to properly care for their own children. One Zulu woman lay on her cot, exhausted. She cried for a lost friend and talked of how she too would soon die, leaving her infected children to await their own deaths. She told me of her father's insistence she return to his village to care for him, a traditional obligation impossible for her to fulfill. When she finished her sad tale I asked her to close her eyes and rest. Opening the sensitive space I held an intention for healing. Among the sensations I felt were those linked to everything she had told me and all I had observed: what I "believed" about her. Each belief stood in the way of the direct experience healing requires. One by one I recognized these concepts and sensations, allowing each to happen until it seemed to dissolve into the whole.

When I was free of the bulk of my prejudice I silently asserted, "I intend for there to be a reduction of pain," and again went through the process of recognizing and allowing new sensations until the space felt equalized. Finally, I "individualized" to her immune system with a further intention for healing. At each stage of this process I couldn't help but momentarily concentrate on the new sensations. The practice was to "de-concentrate," to feel the sensations without focus. Eventually, no one bit of the experience seemed more compelling than any other.

Along the way much of what I felt was of my own creation: sensations coming out of thoughts and preconceptions regarding "AIDS," "woman," "Zulu," "pain," "immune system," and so on. Finally, I felt other sensations, related less to my concepts or thoughts, and more to direct experience. Then, the meditation was no longer about me and my sensations, or even about her and her condition. It was about consciousness itself and the space we shared. For a short time, we transcended individuality and there was no distance between us, no boundary where I ended and she began. For a brief time we existed together in a state of love.

I left her in a deep sleep. Hours later she sought me out and thanked me, over and over. She had relaxed deeply and for the first time in many weeks felt refreshed. There was no cure in this and she has since died, but she did know some peace in the midst of her pain.

With others I have seen release from fear, decreased symptoms, and elimination of disease. Sometimes, in a single session, chronic pain will resolve, acute conditions heal, or negative emotions disappear; all simply a matter of creating an environment in which self-healing can happen. At other times, there is no "cure," only the salve of unconditional love.

Just as you can do this work within yourself and can do healing meditation with others, you can teach others to do healing for themselves. As a counselor, friend, or teacher, guide others to perceive the sensations that precede emotions. It isn't hard. You need only ask them to be still while you verbally guide them in meditation. Have them notice sensations and equalize their awareness. Guide them to feel what they have been afraid to feel and to relax into the raw experience of life.

If you are a helping professional you will find it gratifying to serve others this way. You may already encourage clients to meditate at home but nothing is as effective as bringing meditation directly to the client. Gain experience with your own daily practice: this is the most important thing. Then, as you develop a regular and sincere practice, guide others to do the same.

A good example of this way of working occurred with my client Nancy who had a difficult relationship with her ex-husband. He often demanded she do for their children things he was himself unwilling to do, and Nancy gave in to his wishes over and over. As we talked I could see she was afraid of his anger and was giving in so as to avoid the sensations of it. I asked her to close her eyes and picture a recent time this had happened: to remember when and where, to recall what was said, and hear the way he spoke. I could see by her outward agitation when the memory became real. I guided her to notice the sensations she was having in her body, being sure she distinguished between sensation and emotion. She mentioned a twisted feeling in her stomach and tightness in her throat. She started to tell me how angry she felt but I kept her attention on the sensations themselves. Finally, I asked her to just be with her experience, to practice healing on herself in exactly the same way I had practiced with AIDS patients in Africa. Slowly her agitated movements quieted and after a minute she took a deep inhale, let the breath out with a sigh, and opened her eyes.

I asked her how she was feeling and in a dreamy voice she said: "relaxed." The difficult sensations in her throat and stomach were vaguely familiar but she had learned to avoid them by giving in to her husband. Now, for the first time, she discovered they were quite tolerable (they were, after all, just sensations). They had even become the opening of a pleasant meditation. The vital difference was in her willingness to feel.

After repeating this healing process several times, Nancy was able to face her husband's demands without fear. His anger stirred up the same old sensations but they were tolerable sensations: a small part of her total experience. With this realization came the freedom to say "no." Interestingly, once she did, the demands decreased dramatically and their relationship improved.

Nancy understood why she was afraid of her husband's anger (it reminded her of her father's), why she defended herself in the ways she did (it was the defense she had learned as a little girl), and even why she chose to be married to this man in the first place (partly so she could revisit a place where healing attention was needed). Yet, knowing all this was not enough. Analysis, even of the most sophisticated and penetrating sort, is based on thought and thought cannot easily take one beyond thought. Only when Nancy paused in her thinking and gave herself loving attention was she able to heal the old wounds.

To create true love with all its healing effects, our practice has been to reduce ideas and judgments about the other (or about difficult and alienated parts of ourselves). Those ideas and judgments, more than anything else, keep us separate from one another and fragmented within. Our technique has been to simply feel the sensations we feel when those concepts are present.

Now let's take this practice to a deeper level. Not surprisingly (although this usually goes unrecognized), the person you hold most concepts about is you. You have spent a lifetime amassing ideas, judgments, and concepts to form an elaborate and necessarily limited myth of self, of who and what you think you are. You conceive of yourself as a certain type of person, with certain traits, energy, health, interests, preferences, abilities, disabilities, and so on and on. You carry forward regrets, anger, and guilt as well as pride and attachment, hopes and fears. You formulate this myth of what you are, but only rarely examine the present moment sufficiently to actually know yourself. You believe in this "I" above all else despite the fact that it has no substantive existence.

To experiment with what happens if you eliminate self-concepts you will have to recognize how self-concepts feel. If you think about what a good job you have done on an important project, these thoughts will be felt in a certain way. If it flashes through your mind that you've acted the fool in an important relationship, this will feel some other way. You've already worked with such sensations, to prevent the emotional states they might otherwise stir up. It is a small but delicate further step to be aware of how every notion about self feels a certain way. You'll need to investigate this carefully as it is quite subtle. You have endless ideas, concepts, prejudices, beliefs, and thoughts about yourself, and each generates sensations. Certain themes are ever-present; others vary from day to day, or moment to moment. There are easily recognized ideas such as "I am very intelligent" or "I want a cold beer." Others are more subtle but at least as powerful. You hold beliefs about your potential ("My life is always a struggle"), your inner state ("I am forever hopeful"), and about every other aspect of yourself. These beliefs are usually unarticulated and often obscure but each is experienced as sensation nevertheless. By experiencing these sensations with awareness and perhaps courage you can come into a neutral, loving relationship with the reality of you.

Begin practice by working with some obvious thought about your-self. Think, "I am a (wo)man" or "I am __ years old" and feel the sensa-tions that arise. Don't expect anything dramatic, as this is indeed sub-tle. Allow the sensations with equal attention on all other sensations of the moment, until the sensations blend into overall awareness and your consciousness is equalized. When you are neutral move on to another concept. Again, reduce any tendency to concentrate and simply be aware. Continue in this way, proceeding to more and more subtle beliefs. Be sure to include the negative or limited. Finally, you will come to the sense of your individuality, the sensations related to "I am."

With care and diligence you can come to know self, to recognize it at work and comprehend its drives. Moreover, you can neutralize any of its negative effects on consciousness. You will need to practice to dis-cover the consequences of this awareness. This would be a good time to begin.

$$\$\$\$\$\$$$

Our practice is going beyond the common idea of meditation. Most students have no difficulty understanding stillness, awareness, and courage (and most meditation instruction lets off right about there) but some are taken aback by the notion that meditative presence can be healing for others or lessen the grip of ego within. As we con-tinue we'll look into a consciousness in which the divide between self and other, observer and observed, begins to be erased. Where there is no division, there is wholeness; and just as you can experience compas-sion and healing when you reduce separation between self and other, so you can create self-love, self-healing, and self-compassion when you reduce division within. These are the consequences of sincere practice.

The essence of meditation is no effort. Meditation is not about "personal growth" and it is never wise to enter into practice striving for self-improvement. Meditation is how we realize what we are; it is not about becoming something better. Even with an intention to heal we're not saying, "This is how things are but they should be this other way and I'm going to fix it." We only declare that we intend to be in an effortless relation to what is. Our meditation includes no preferences, no ego, none of the stuff of the little self. When we maintain effortless being, immersed in experience, negative ego isn't there to muck things up and whatever needs to happen can.

But why meditate if not to accomplish something? Even if there is no goal, how does one escape hoping to have no desires or striving to be at peace? I actually can't answer that. It's a problem we each face and you will need to work it out for yourself.

Even meditation teachers may not understand this. They often recommend bringing the mind under control and suggest the way to do so is to observe the mind, noting thoughts and emotions as they arise, and letting them go. There are three pitfalls in this approach that can create difficulties in further practice. The first is making effort to control the mind. Certainly it's out of control, filled with all sorts of emotion and thought, but only if you stop trying to control it can you experience mind as it is, and only then can there be acceptance and peace with who or what you actually are. If you try to control your mind, it is always with the assumption there is something wrong with it, and practice based on such self-criticism won't go very far.

The second pitfall is in the opposite effort to "let go" of thought or emotion. Why? What harm might follow if we allowed ourselves to be and to feel exactly what is present in this moment? We don't want to overindulge in thought or emotion but if we allow the sensations of these to be felt they are likely to be of some value. They do, after all, indicate precisely where attention is needed.

The third pitfall is the most insidious. Establishing an observer within, one who watches the rest of you, creates a duality. It might be fascinating to watch your mind with disinterest, from a slightly removed vantage point, but to do so perpetuates separation: a neutral and steady observer watching over a wandering and perhaps foolish thinker. Instead of observing the mind, experiment with allowing the mind to experience itself, just as it is. Don't be letting go of anything. Be neutral, unattached, and highly aware, but not even a little distant.

Healing

Pause now to practice again. Investigate how it feels to observe the self or to pass judgment. You are so used to these things you may have difficulty discerning how they affect you but they are right there, near the center of consciousness, and they affect everything. Feel the slight but pervasive sensations of "I am," "This is great," or "That's me." Spend plenty of time with this practice: it is subtle and important and something to return to throughout life.

———————————— §§§§§ ————————————

Perhaps the most powerful question you can ask, especially in times of distress or discord, is "What is the most healing, loving, and compassionate thing to do right now?" Prior to doing these practices you might have thought of loving action as giving of something: a gift, a kind word, attentive listening, affection, an apology, or loving thoughts. These are marvelous, of course, but the most loving thing might be to hold the healing space, remove "self" from the picture, and allow the experience to flow. This seems to produce the greatest joy. Love and compassion are, literally, at the heart of meditation and happiness. It is good to understand this but it is far better to practice. Practice a little each day, reducing concepts about self and others and be a healer in the world.

A Meditation for Compassion and the Capacity to Heal

Compassion, healing, and love are manifestations of a heart in balance. This meditation, also taught by Yogi Bhajan, balances the heart chakra. The instructions require careful attention but the meditation itself is easy.

Sit with a straight spine, elbows down and tucked into the ribs. Forearms are straight up and wrists bent so the palms face up and are flat and parallel to the floor, pointing forward at 45°. Keep the fingers together but the thumbs out, pointing behind you. You want there to be some tension as you maintain this position. Avoid curling your hands or fingers. This brings healing energy from the heart into your hands, with which you touch the world. Your eyes will be closed and focused at the third eye.

The mantra is magnificent: Raa Maa Daa Saa, Saa Say So Hung. All the syllables are drawn out except Hung, which is clipped short. Raa, the sun, Maa, the moon: these are the two polarities of Infinity. Daa, the earth, receiver of all. Saa is the totality, the Infinite. Saa Say So Hung declares, "I am this Infinity." Together it establishes that all energies are in you, as in all creation; and you are an integral element within a timeless flow.

Inhale deeply and chant the mantra in a pleasing monotone on one breath, taking five or more seconds to do so. On the first Saa sound, pull in and up on your navel point (three finger widths below the belly button), giving the sound extra emphasis, and then release. Pull and release the navel point again as you make the sound So.

Practice this mantra for eleven to thirty one minutes. To finish, take a deep inhale. Hold the breath in as you consciously include in your healing space whomever you wish. Exhale after fifteen seconds or so and repeat this two more times. ◎

GRATITUDE:
Loving Life Exactly As It Is

"Life is not for wasting. It is for reaching the wonderlands of your own consciousness."
  - Yogi Bhajan

Yogi Bhajan often exhorted his students to develop an "attitude of gratitude." After studying with him for a year or so, my wife and I asked Yogiji for a spiritual name. He said, "You are Subagh," which means "fortunate" or "blessed." I remember some shock as he said this. His words flew in the face of my tendency to think that my life was never quite good enough.

A few weeks later, my wife went into labor after only six months of pregnancy and the baby was stillborn. Holding the tiny body, chanting a mantra to help the little one's soul on its journey, I suddenly understood: we were blessed. This event, awful though it might have been, brought us into an intimate relation with reality, to something beyond all ego or personal choice. The experience was intense and painful but there was nothing to do but surrender to it. With that surrender came a unique and unexpected peace. The peace was real, not just based on some philosophical concept. We were blessed even in this inexplicable sadness, and I was genuinely grateful, not for what had happened, but for the capacity to feel it all, exactly as it was.

Earlier lessons have examined how a neutral relationship with the pain of difficult experience can give one peace and freedom from suffering (which is always the result of wishing we didn't have to feel the pain). We've also seen how one can experience pleasure without the suffering of attachment.

Now these same skills will form the basis for the practice of gratitude. If you can work with the arduous or the distasteful and use it to elevate yourself, it is no great stretch to be grateful for the opportunity to do so and even to be grateful for the difficulties themselves. Emotions, attachments, fears, desires, and all the rest can be put to good use. The ways we make our own lives difficult can be turned around and used to recapture the liberation and happiness of our original selves.

Have you ever noticed how often you find yourself in the midst of familiar difficulties? We repeat negative patterns and repeatedly get into the same sort of mess with the same old challenges and conflicts. It seems that our highest purpose is not to avoid these difficulties but to learn from them. When we've learned our lessons the old difficulties disappear and we can move on to new challenges. Our highest need is to finally get it right.

I see repeating patterns in me and in all of my clients. One woman, Jean, is typical. She's the daughter of a father whose mood swings frightened and angered her when she was a child. Jean came to me after another long-term relationship had failed. Each of her partners had also been moody. She wanted a committed relationship but was afraid of again being victim to a partner's moods. She said, in effect, "Either I have to be alone and lonely, or I have to be in a painful partnership."

The question was what happened before her fear and anger appeared, in the important instant between a partner's mood shift and the appearance of her emotions. This was the pain she was avoiding and the place that needed healing. I guided her into meditation and asked her to imagine a typical situation: to see and hear her partner as he went through his changes and to notice exactly what sensations began to appear. She recognized a familiar fear and also something she had never noticed before: a sinking feeling, a heaviness in her chest, a weight on her shoulders, a sick feeling in her throat. I asked her to allow these sensations, without resistance, as well as any other sensations that appeared. Soon she relaxed a bit and said with some heaviness, "I'll never get it right." This belief, this thought, was her own creation, but the fear and sinking feeling which proceeded it by a split second was her actual experience, and they had become inextricably linked.

Once Jean paused long enough to notice all this she begin healing. It went more or less like the other examples I've given and I needn't detail how she gradually became more able to feel her pain. The healing she experienced was not only in her relationships but also in a very deep part of her. She gradually became able, for the first time since childhood, to live without self-doubt. As she did, other aspects of her life also improved. If it hadn't been for the pain of her adult relationships her old wounds might never have been healed, and this is the point of her story.

In meditation there is a full allowing of each moment's sensations. This inherently leads us to a peaceful place, which is where we want to be. Emotional pain, when actually felt, is not a problem to be eliminated but a doorway into the realm of peace. Pain is useful, a signpost pointing the way. Without it and those who "caused" the pain, we would never have these opportunities to heal and find deeper happiness.

Many people seem "happy enough" yet maintain foggy corners in consciousness: places where part of the experience of now is obscured. They may be functional, successful people but still be plagued by the effects of unacknowledged pain. Lasting happiness won't emerge if there are interior places unvisited, or painful sensations unfelt. Without gratitude for the fullness of now you may close a door on further learning and escape again into distractions, addictions, and negative emotions.

As you meditate with courage and love you create "perfect moments," moments in which you transmute suffering into harmonious being. You can be grateful for having this ability just as you are grateful for the difficulties making it necessary. Without both you might never notice this moment's perfection. The implications are great. If you can appreciate such a moment, it means you have been prepared to do so. You've had the teachers and experience, the courage and awareness, the will and resources to elevate yourself. Somehow,

Gratitude

all your past experience has led you to this moment and you are able to feel peace and joy. With this hindsight you can see how nothing was ever "wrong" and so there is nothing to forgive.

Of course, I don't celebrate any abuse or pain you might have known or believe you shouldn't take steps to prevent these in the future. However, if they are present now or have been in your past you're fully empowered to use them for your benefit. Forgiveness is only necessary if, instead of putting pain to good use, we try to put it behind us. Forgiveness is for those who still wish the past had been different, who still can't or won't come to peace, within their selves. To one with a devoted and developed practice, resentment evaporates and forgiveness becomes unnecessary. This is not necessarily easy, but it is always possible, a choice that can be made.

I am not suggesting that you should tolerate severe pain with an obvious cause in present time. When I was a teenager my leg was crushed in a run-in between my bike and a truck. While the truck was still parked on my leg there was nothing but pain filling every bit of consciousness and demanding immediate action. The only thing was for the truck to get off me; and I was completely uninterested in coming to peace until it did. We have to understand our priorities.

Outer conditions are often wrong. It is wrong when a child is abused, when an employee is exploited, when the natural world is raped to satisfy corporate greed. It's possibly wrong if a relationship disintegrates or one contracts a serious illness. But our actual sensations are never wrong. Our most difficult sensations (again, not our emotions) are there to awaken us and direct our awareness to what most needs attention.

After all these words, it is time once again for practice. Sit for meditation, tune in, and create a space of stillness and awareness. Within your meditation repeatedly express gratitude for whatever experience you might be having right now, regardless of what it includes, and without any evaluation of this experience. Simply feel the conditions of now using all your skills of stillness, awareness, and courage. Feel the little itches, your sore back, the pain of harbored resentment, the pleasant relaxation of tense muscles, the temperature of your skin, or anything else that appears. Equalize awareness and then, silently or aloud, offer your thanks over and over. Saying "thank you" implies a "you" to whom the thanks are offered. You may prefer "I am grateful." Use whatever feels natural. You needn't think of reasons to be grateful or review the philosophy of this lesson. All of this is somewhere in the back of your mind, giving you confidence in the rightness of gratitude. Continue this meditation for eleven minutes or more and return to it often.

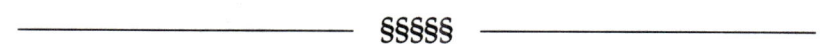

§§§§§

When you practice gratitude deeply and consistently three precious qualities arise. First, you feel gratitude for the past that brought you to this moment. Second, you know compassion for the present in which nothing is shunned and no one is a problem. Third, you take responsibility for the future, choosing to live this moment "perfectly" so as to create only helpful and healing effects. These three qualities are among the marks of a liberated person.

Gratitude

A Meditation for Gratitude

Gratitude is associated with the throat chakra, from which we communicate, express ourselves, and inspire others. Practice of the following meditation taught by Yogi Bhajan will help to create balance in this area so gratitude can flow.

Tune in. Sit straight, with hands resting on your knees in Gyan Mudra: tips of thumb and index finger touching while other fingers are straight but relaxed; and palms face up. This finger position creates subtle effects in consciousness, stimulating and blending wisdom and understanding.

The key to this meditation is for your neck to be in what is called neck lock. In this your chin is pulled back towards the notch between the collarbones but the neck is straight with no forward tilt of your head. Your chest is out, heart center expanded and lifted. The position is as if you were at attention, but relaxed. Keep the pressure on this "lock" and chant the mantra "Humee Hum, Brahm Hum." The neck position will cause you to chant in a way that uses the back of the tongue more than is usual, creating a throaty sound. Throughout the meditation (do it for eleven minutes) keep your eyes opened and focused on the tip of your nose. Feel the mantra vibrating in your throat. Like all the other meditations, this one can be practiced every day for 40 or more days, or used whenever you feel the need to reconnect with your sense of gratitude.

◎

DEVOTION:
To Perfection

"The limits of human beings are their fears and their unlimited power is their inspiration. When you concentrate inspiration, it is called faith."
- Yogi Bhajan

We need to start this lesson by clarifying what "devotion" means. There are at least three types. The first could also be called discipline. You might be devoted to a code of ethics, developing a new skill, or beginning each day with yoga and meditation. Such devotion, to practicing even when it is difficult to do so, is always valuable.

A second sort of devotion is to a known object: some person, thing, or event within one's own experience. Devotion to a teacher, a social cause, or a spiritual community would all fit in this category. While these are often part of a rich spirituality they do carry the risk of blind faith and the fanaticism that can breed, so devotion of this sort needs to be carefully considered. Nevertheless, these first two varieties of devotion are easy enough to understand. They are based on personal experience and, hopefully, on well-considered commitments.

A third type of devotion is to the unknown or unsubstantiated. Devotion to a deity, an historic prophet, an unverified belief, or a point of dogma are the common examples. This devotion does not include direct personal experience with, or verification of, the object of devotion and thus must be founded on faith. To be devoted in this way one must "believe in" something, something that remains, for the present at least, unknown. This, of course, is the foundation of most religious practice and can be extremely valuable. Faith-based devotion often inspires lasting discipline and good works and occasionally leads to transcendence. However, with devotion of this third kind we skate on rather thin ice in a realm where devotion can become problematic in two significant ways.

First, if one claims devotion to "God," for example, but has no direct experience of that mystery one will tend to rely on beliefs about God. Beliefs, like any concepts, act as filters. They may distort perception and inappropriately interpose intellect and actually limit one's ability to have a direct, unbiased experience of the unlimited. This is true of any such object of devotion, in any faith tradition.

Second, in many faiths devotion is to a god believed to be remote, unknowable, and definitely supreme. Devotees perceive themselves as separate from and inferior to a magnificent other. This sense of separation and inequality can permeate both faith and culture. All too easily everything is perceived as either divine or worldly, saved or damned, good or evil, friend or enemy. It is obvious what enormous suffering this continues to cause. It is the very opposite of the integration and wholeness needed if we are to heal the world.

Similarly, one can fall prey to an imagined and parallel separation within: a separation into those aspects of self that are felt to be good and those that are not. Personal healing and happiness, like healing of the larger world, is also the consequence of integration and a sense of wholeness. If I were to believe something about me was wrong and needed to be eliminated or corrected in order for me to be a better person, I might very well divide against myself; one part judging and condemning the other. In much the same way those who see the world in terms of good and evil may seek destruction of, rather than reconciliation with, the "enemy."

Our practice of devotion must transcend such limitations, regardless of our faith. Faith is fine and often valuable but blind faith is not. We need to practice so as to reduce separation, increase wholeness, and have direct experience of reality. In the beginning just one bit of faith is required: a small belief in the potential of practice. There is no way around this if we wish to get started.

The practice of devotion based on meditation has but two interrelated aspects. The first will use everything you have learned up to this point. Begin your meditation with stillness and awareness. Sometimes it is useful to begin with awareness of one small but vivid particle of your experience. Recognize how the sensations of it appear in you. Then, with equalized awareness include more and more sensations of now, expanding consciousness until it seems to include everything. When you feel stable in this, begin to also allow sensations associated with "I," "me," and "mine:" the subtle sensations of a separate self. This is a simple practice but it will require steadiness in your meditation. It may take time for the individual point of view drop away, leaving not "your" experience but experience, existence, itself.

This state of no self has been called many things, but none of them begin to describe it. It is not that you will disappear, just that you can, from time to time, experience the universe through the original, transpersonal self, not running everything through filters of accumulated idea, belief, fear, desire, emotion, and thought. When the ego-self is gently set down there is room for totally fresh wisdom and spontaneity. Possibly, pure bliss or a sense of Oneness, of knowing God-in-all may appear. This is what daily practice does. It lets us sample that greater awareness. In the aftermath of such experience you find yourself devoted to this sensational and known phenomenon with no further effort.

---

§§§§§

The other aspect of devotion practice is recollection of the divine, most commonly through the repetition of mantra, a "name of God," an expression or sound reflecting elevated consciousness. These mantras are like hints, small clues to an unlimited reality. Masters blessed with transcendent awareness have understood God as the all-in-all, a presence permeating creation and beyond. Some have given It names: The One, Sat Nam, Wahe Guru, Om, Hari, God, Rama, Allah, Creator, Absolute, Divine Mother, and countless others, and these names are mantras. Other mantras are succinct phrases about the transcendent or our relation to it ("God and me, me and God, are one" is a favorite of mine) or are references or prayers to divine beings ("Lord Jesus Christ, have mercy on me"). Mantras are not merely sounds or words. When uttered with sensitivity they echo the very vibration of sacredness. Mantra is mental purification and mantra meditation is like spring cleaning for the mind. (Mantra practice is almost universal although many faiths use longer or more complex prayers or chants. It is best to learn these practices from teachers within those traditions.)

Mantra practice can help us remember our wholeness, and give us a way to express and manifest it. With mantras we connect to our already enlightened nature and have a way to declare that connection. When you've entered a sacred space, as in the last meditation, a mantra can express and recall your experience. Mantra and the sacred become one and the same, inextricably linked in consciousness. By repeating a mantra during meditation it becomes associated with your clearest moments. Subsequent repetition of the sound helps you remember or conjure up your highest experience.

If you are ill or distressed and wrapped up in "me," you can easily compound your own difficulties. You need to care for yourself but break patterns of self-absorption. The surest way is to chant a mantra, letting it take over the mental space occupied by worries. Mantra will help dispel confusion and return you to peace. A little discipline is required of course, but when used sincerely mantras are powerful tools.

A mantra is like a faithful friend, always there when needed, in good times and bad. Of the things of this world, only a mantra and the pure consciousness it represents will never fail you. No matter how much you and a loved one are attached to one another, one of you might depart in an instant. No matter what diversions occupy you, they can be taken away. No matter how vital or energized you feel today, your body will eventually decay. Everything you accumulate will be left behind. But in every circumstance, even at the moment of death, mantra can remain with you. "God's name" is the one thing it is wise to attach to.

To begin mantra practice, chose one from the list on page 15 or from another source. Any mantra you feel drawn to will serve. Sit in meditation, reducing self-centeredness in the same way you did in the last exercise. Bring yourself to a clear and stable awareness and begin to repeat the mantra in time with your breathing. Some mantras easily divide into two halves so you can repeat half of it as you inhale and half as you exhale; or you can repeat the whole mantra as you inhale, and repeat it again as you exhale.

This linkage of mantra and breath is particularly valuable. Breath is always with you. With continued practice mantra can be experienced with each breath. Even when your mind is occupied with other thoughts the mantra will remain there, at the center of all experience. This single practice, this continuous recollection of the divine in all, this remembering God, is the ultimate practice.

If you want to chant aloud, which is especially powerful, take a deep inhale and slowly chant as you exhale. In general, stretch out the vowel sounds, touch the tip of your tongue to the back of your palate when the sound allows, and feel the vibration in throat, nose, and palate. A qualified teacher can guide you further, but these are the essentials.

As you continue in meditation, substitute the mantra for thoughts or emotions as they are noticed. If you realize you've drifted off, return to the mantra. If you need to do this a hundred times, don't worry, just do it. Include any sensations your wanderings engender, and return to the mantra. You're not trying to stop thought but only to substitute a precious thought of the divine for each more mundane thought you notice.

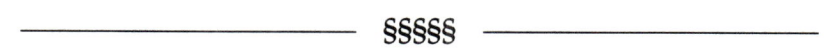

§§§§§

In your practice the sense of self will tend to diminish or drop away. On a subtle level you draw a connection between the mantra and that meditative experience. Subsequent repetition of the mantra will help bring you back to that place you have already found in yourself. In this way your devotion practice (repetition of mantra) will be to a known thing (your own elevated consciousness) and neither striving for self-improvement nor blind faith will enter the picture. Over time, the experience will deepen. Your mantra will help you to quickly enter the meditative space and discover more of your own reality. Then you'll have still more profound experience to link mantra to, and so on.

For simplicity's sake I've separated devotion into two aspects and written of mantras as if they were merely code words but neither reflects actual practice. Mantra repetition is how we call upon the Infinite, ask it to embrace us, and express limitless joy upon knowing that embrace, but I can't describe such experience or guide you further. It is up to each of us to practice sincerely, confident that the masters have pointed out a true path, and discover for ourselves what may come of it. The deepest devotion is based on personal experience and you need to provide that for yourself.

As you go about your busy day continuously choose to let mundane things of the mind give way to your mantra. If you notice emotions, put the mantra in the place where the emotion was. If you are daydreaming, replace your musings with the mantra. If you feel delight, celebrate and go beyond delight with mantra practice. Slowly, let the sacredness of mantra substitute for the mundane and become an ever-present friend, a reminder of the object of life, and an expression of your true nature. What happens as a result of these devotions is not under your control. You don't do this, or any other practice, so as to achieve some new goal; you do it to awaken to who you are. There is a fine line here. Somehow we each have to discover how to practice effortlessly, without desire, and to let whatever happens, happen.

I once adopted a dog from the local pound. When he first saw me he pressed against the side of his cage, getting as close to me as possible. I was unable to resist his instant devotion, his attempt to close the gap between us, and in minutes he was mine. Mantra practice is like that, a way of pressing ourselves as close as possible to the thin veil separating our limited consciousness from an unlimited consciousness, expecting, any time now, to be taken home by this new Master.

Devotion, of course, can also be manifested through prayer. One can think of prayer as the process of focusing the mind and mentally addressing the Infinite. In contrast, one can think of meditation as clearing the mind of all that is limited so that one can become aware of the Unlimited. I'm not going to examine prayer here as it falls outside of the scope of this book.

A Meditation for Deepening Devotion

Devotion is associated with the energy and awareness in the area where the top of the nose joins the skull, the sixth chakra. This is the region relating to intuition, the elevation of thought, the brain and pituitary, and so on. Practice of the following meditation from the teachings of Yogi Bhajan will help "open" the third eye and give you a clearer awareness of sacred reality. It will enhance your ability to know the unknown and see the unseen and thus bring you to a place where devotion is completely natural.

Sit with a straight spine, as in other meditations. With eyes open and unblinking, look down at the tip of your nose. Your eyes will cross a little and at first there may be slight fatigue in the eye muscles. Use any mantra, repeated either aloud or silently, in time with your breath. Keep up for eleven minutes. You may want to experiment with doing this meditation every day, sometime between four and eight a.m., for forty consecutive days.

The Seventh Lesson

SURRENDER:
Letting Go of All Effort

"The fact is that there is nothing more beautiful, more worthy, or more conscious than you."
    - Yogi Bhajan

Some years ago I retired after twenty-five years as a dentist. A new stage of life was about to begin and I sought vision in a remote valley in the Jemez Mountains of New Mexico. For three days I alternated chanting, silent meditation, and short naps, eating nothing and taking only occasional sips from a spring-fed pool. I had been attached to the idea of receiving guidance but these had been three very empty days. When it was time for me to leave my hideaway I felt disappointed by the lack of insight. Clearing my head with a quick walk around the campsite I sat for one last meditation. I felt myself giving up hope for this to be a special time and surrendered to the situation as it was. Just then my meditation deepened and a single word leapt to mind. The word was "suniae" which in the language of the Sikhs means listening, in the sense of "communion with God." Suniae begins line after line near the beginning of our sacred text, the Siri Guru Granth Sahib. In translation a few of those lines read:

Listening, one immerses in an ocean of virtue.
Listening, one becomes a religious teacher, a spiritual guide,
        and a divine ruler.
Listening, even the spiritually blind can find their path.
Listening, the Unknowable can be grasped.

Surrender

O Nanak! God's devoted lovers are forever in bliss.
Listening, all suffering and error vanishes.

Three days of fasting and meditating while holding on to hope and desire had led to nothing. Then, three minutes of surrender gave me more than I could have hoped for. Suniae, virtually a one-word scripture connoting stillness, awareness, devotion, and surrender has guided me in life and practice ever since.

Surrender, like devotion, is often misunderstood. We think of hope as a virtue. We're attached to individualism and getting our own way. We set goals, believe in the efficacy of hard work, and object to the very idea of giving up personal prerogatives. Even in this book it has been hard to avoid suggesting that a practice might lead to a particular effect. But we can't put it off any longer. We've come to the point where all remnants of hope and desire must be abandoned. It is time to let off trying and surrender the mind to the soul.

Surrender is not something you accomplish. It is the very fine art of doing nothing while holding yourself in a sensitive or sacred space, through the use of mantra or other practices. You've actually begun already. In practicing devotion you surrendered self so as to have authentic experience. Being still required surrendering urges to move. Awareness called for surrendering preferences and concepts in order to simply feel. Gratitude is about surrendering demands for things to be a certain way, and so on. With these practices you have begun the process of letting go of hope and desire. The question now is: how does one surrender completely, unshackling oneself from the urge to improve conditions and even from the insistence on being an individual, separate unto oneself?

Working towards surrender is absurd and simply choosing surrender is not so easy. Surrender requires a lot while paradoxically demanding you do nothing at all. In the everyday world of school or career you need to get things done, set goals, and bring them to fruition, but if you choose to enter into the rarefied world of mystic practice you will, in your meditations at least, need to set such things aside.

For our specialized purposes we need to let go of all attempts to change and enter instead a state of openness to being what we actually are. In this is great humility. If we set out to achieve a particular state of being, no matter how spiritual or ethical or virtuous our goal may be, we separate from ourselves, from who we are now. If I am motivated to be good, does my motivation create goodness or just more desire? Can an urge in my mind based on desire take me beyond desire and allow me to be free? Real goodness has no motive, because all motivation is based on needs and desires. Real goodness, real humility, only appears where there is simple attention, or "suniae." This is never attention so as to get something.

Spiritual urges are no different from other urges. They are based on a self you want to improve, one with a continuous history, perceived flaws, and a hoped for future. It is possible, for example, to use prayer, yoga, and meditation in much the same way one might use drugs, materialistic acquisition, or therapy: as nothing more than a way to improve how one feels. Of course, there are useful drugs, helpful possessions, and good therapies, just as prayer, yoga, and meditation can serve one's highest purposes. The point is to avoid using any of these things in place of simple, surrendered awareness.

Begin to understand practice and effort as a way to let go of effort, as a prelude to surrender. Try (without trying, of course) to find that peaceful place. You may have come to this book with an urge for change. We all begin with this and practice accordingly, whether in spiritual realms or in the material world. But there must finally come a time when even our most virtuous urges are released. When they are, there is a possibility of the ultimate healing of awakening and merger. Outwardly, nothing changes, but inwardly there can be a radical shift unlike anything in previous experience. With hard-earned skills we become liberated, approach the Divine, and then utterly relinquish all desire for more. The shift we make is into a state in which we are willing to allow this, forever if need be; a state of absolute humility and zero effort on behalf of the personal self. This state, this surrender, opens us to all other possibilities.

So, how does one do this? Recall the subtle practice of recognizing what the sense of self feels like in you. Begin to incorporate this into all your meditations, continually recognizing the experience of "I" and the sensations of self. Because these sensations are subtle you will likely slide in and out of this awareness many times. Keep up and your ability to be stable will grow. As it does you will be "healing" this concept of self. Then it can move, as all things move when not held tightly. Self is not based on anything concrete and begins to dissolve as soon as you break your attachment to it. This is surrender and here is where things begin to get very interesting.

For virtually your entire life you've been dedicated to preserving this I-am-ness, this self, at all costs. And yet, this self is not a fixed entity. It only exists if you maintain it in consciousness. If there is no reference to past or future, and if you release "I," "Me," and "Mine,"the personal self simply fades away. When it does, a grander reality can appear. Just as an electron can sometimes appear as particle, sometimes as wave, you also have a dual nature, appearing sometimes as ego-centered and separate and sometimes as transpersonal and interconnected with all that is.

Pause again for a meditation, one in which you heal the sense of self. Bear in mind that the sensations are likely to be subtle. They won't shock you like a stubbed toe. You might have a thought of self ("I need to go to the store") and not notice particular sensations at all. The idea is not to go looking for something special but only to return continuously to feeling this moment's experience, with the intention of reducing self.

§§§§§

We feel a need for a separate identity, with its limited sense of what we are and what we do, in order to function in the everyday world, but we can also experience reality without these filters of identity. From time to time, at least within meditation, the ego-self can be surrendered. As you continue this long-term project of examining and releasing limited concepts of self, avoid replacing them with new "improved" concepts. Instead, practice with no conditions; surrendering any new self and any new desires you might conjure up. Examine and release hopes of becoming like some new, improved ideal; otherwise the restricting falseness of ego will continue to plague you.

The antagonist of surrender, which makes it seem so hard, is becoming, the perpetual wish to be what we are not. You are alone and want to have a lover; I am sick and am trying to become well. Another is a sinner and hopes to become a saint. All this becoming, even of the most positive sort, is stifling. Striving drags on the spirit, as it is based on not loving who you already are. Real love needs no improvement; it only needs surrender.

A Meditation for Surrender

Surrender is a function of the seventh chakra, located at the crown of the head. Here, above all thought and emotion, there can be a direct communion with the Universal. Yogi Bhajan gave this "Meditation on Ecstasy" to help us to drop the self-conscious mind and immerse ourselves in the Infinite, clearing away the urge to become.

Sit in meditation posture with hands in gyan mudra and eyes closed. Inhale deeply and chant the mantra Wa-hay Guru, Wa-hay Guru, Wa-hay Wa-hay Wa-hay Guru on one breath. Chant in a monotone for eleven minutes, then inhale deeply and hold the breath while concentrating the energy at the top of your head. After thirty seconds exhale and relax. Wa-hay Guru expresses ecstasy and wonder at the perfection of this. Listen to the sounds you are making and let them connect you with a divine sound within. Practicing this for forty consecutive days will be particularly powerful.

◎

MERGER:
Awakening to All You Are

"You are here to serve, to uplift, to be graceful, to give hope, and to give the very deep love of your soul to all those in need. Through service you can win the world."
   - *Yogi Bhajan*

As we've gone through these lessons the practices have perhaps become more difficult. In the last lesson the instructions were to do nothing, which is indeed difficult to master. I suggested that transcendence could only come about under conditions of surrender and no effort. So now, as we investigate merger, what further guidance could there possibly be?

First, please realize that the word merger (or enlightenment, or awakening, or whatever you might call it) is almost useless (although I am going to use it nevertheless). It might hint at a bit of the experience or point a direction, but ultimately it's misleading. I'm not a poet and haven't a prayer of getting it right. Merger, or any other element of mystical consciousness, can't be described. We use a word like "surrender" or "awareness" and think we understand surrender and awareness, but these words are like so many concepts: ideas about experience but not the experience itself, the map but certainly not the territory.

In fact, the territory of merger, experienced in what has been called the super-conscious, is completely uncharted. It's not that others haven't been awakened; it's just that they haven't drawn maps. Instead, the great masters have given us metaphors and, more importantly, practices, ways we can approach super-consciousness. If we practice in those ways, and surrender, we might possibly find ourselves transformed. But there are no step-by-step instructions because at the end there are no "steps" to be taken. What happens is a kind of quantum leap: first you are here and then you are there, with no path in between. It's not so rare, actually. If you practice sincerely and diligently, you're likely to experience many such moments of sacred awareness. The real trick is to recognize that space and become stable in it. That's what takes practice.

Although awakening might arise out of practice and surrender, it's never planned. There aren't even definite prerequisites. Practice seems to be of value but many have had profound enlightenment experiences without any apparent effort and others have practiced diligently for decades without a single moment of transcendence. It's out of our hands. The only thing seems to be to keep up, maintaining practice free from desire, without expectation, and even without hope.

Some time ago, after I had practiced many years, I saw how much I had not practiced: how little I had been willing to surrender and how goal-driven my practice had been. In the center of practice there had remained desire. Over time, my desires had evolved and I was concerned with being a better person and doing more good; but even these ambitions were a continual source of anxiety and discomfort. I was troubled by desire but it also motivated me and so I remained unwilling to surrender my desire, fearing that might lead to a bland existence without purpose or meaning.

I began to feel empty and found less and less inspiration in everyday life. Looking for a way out, I thought to practice courage, taking on the oppressive sensations, drawing them in as if I treasured them, and releasing resistance. Slowly they lost some of their power and I began to feel more alive, aware of more than those heavy sensations.

In this new state I released the urge to puzzle out what to do, realizing answers couldn't come from an anxious mind. In the place previously occupied by futile worries I began to practice devotion, meditating on the mantra Guru, Guru, Wa-hay Guru, Guru Ram Das Guru. ("Wise, wise, wise beyond description is the one who serves God" or "Wise beyond description is my Guru, Guru Ram Das.") Guru Ram

Das, the fourth Sikh Guru, lived in India in the sixteenth century. He was the perfect healer, giving over his entire life to service, blessing countless others with his presence. As I began meditating on him, drawing his spirit and example to myself, I recalled another meditation, one I hadn't practiced for a year or more. The thought came as an instruction: "Practice this way." The meditation is one in which one blesses others. (See page 84)

As I began the practice I was reminded of an old teaching, one Yogi Bhajan summed up in an interesting phrase. He said, "If you can fake it, you can make it." He didn't mean one should pretend to be great or hold oneself out as something one was not. He meant that we can chose, right now, to bless and heal others and to be fully present, in the manner of a true master. Because we have been given these practices and because we are already perfect, we can make a gesture from our perfect center, an act of faith, a recognition of our Buddha nature, a tacit acknowledgement of our enlightened self.

There is no pretense in this, nor is it an empty gesture. It simply calls up an aspect of our being which may have been hidden in a fog of unknowing but has always been there, nevertheless. When we choose to heal or bless another we necessarily set aside ego, recognizing that what we call God is in all, and all are in that God. In healing or blessing we are choosing to get out of the way so something beyond the self might prevail.

This is a legitimate choice, "faking it" only from the point of view of the limited ego. Certainly each and every soul comes fully equipped to serve in such a way. To the awakened mind, blessings given are quite natural, emanating as they do from a place beyond limitation. You have the capacity to give such blessings just as you have the capacity to heal. It may seem a stretch if your practice is weak but with reasonable diligence you can begin to imagine yourself as unlimited. When you do and take a little leap of faith, you can perform miracles, acting as if you were merged in the divine, which of course you are.

So, there is a practice beyond surrender after all. After surrender, there is this other way, this acting as a master, a healer, a realized one. By acting the part you experience something new. In this very moment you can pause, feel the sensations of this experience, express your gratitude and devotion, and surrender still further. Then, from this place you can choose to bless and heal others.

We haven't entered into this project of liberation and healing just for us. Had you thought you would be satisfied with simply being free? What you do from now on, whether it be this new way of healing or some other good work or whatever service you've already been offering, can be infused with this acting "as if" you were awakened.

It all comes down to this: there is tremendous suffering in the world. We need to relieve it and help to bring about a great revolution in human consciousness. The only sure way is with love. Many efforts can be made: we can feed and house the poor, educate new generations to live gently on the earth, help people to help themselves, even learn to defend ourselves and others if that proves necessary. These are essential things, but if they are done without love they may be destructive or desperate or shallow at best. Love is not an attitude, something you force upon yourself or others as a duty. Love and healing are practices within oneself and whomever you include in your awakened consciousness. Engaged in these practices, manifesting love as an enlightened one would, you embrace an already enlightened self.

Thus, even though one must surrender all effort to transcend boundaries of ego and arrive in an enlightened place, one can act as if one had already arrived. This is neither an imponderable paradox, nor a slick trick. It is no more nor less than an act of faith in one's self, one of the very few acts of faith ever required. When you bless or heal another you honor the God-in-you and in the other. If all of this nudges you inexorably towards awakening, so be it. That is not your concern. Just give because it is what an enlightened one does, and how one can help heal and bring greater wisdom into the world.

You are not alone. In the midst of all the chaos and painful confusion in the world there also are growing numbers dedicated to peace and harmonious living. Something new is happening. We are still on the fringes but our numbers are growing and what we are bringing into the world is clearly better for all. There will come a tipping point, a moment in time when we catalyze an explosion of loving, universal consciousness. At that moment there will be reason to believe our fragile planet can be saved. You are an important part of this movement.

Each of us, in creating a focus of peace and awareness is interconnected with all others. Our love and healing are blessings for all of us, with greater ramifications than we may realize, perhaps with ramifications even greater than we can realize.

There is only one pitfall, what could be called "spiritual ego." As we work in these realms, the tendency is to think we are pretty special. It's a common problem and painful to witness. People discover this healing power we all have and believe it is their unique gift, something to set them apart from the common folk. It pollutes the healing space and perpetuates the separation we intend to reduce. Where there is separation, there can also appear power, exploitation, and feelings of superiority. Do be careful.

Now you have it all. In every essential way you have the capacity to liberate yourself and live in happiness, unaffected by the vicissitudes of life. You have ways of serving the world as a master and, I pray, you have the patience and inspiration to keep up at your practice during the darkest hours and the most glorious. It doesn't get any better than this.

Here are two more meditations for you to practice. The first meditation is a way to bless others. The second is a way to recognize your merger in the Infinite. Practice these things sincerely. Their combined power might just have remarkable effects on you life.

Merger

A Meditation for Blessing Others

Begin, as always, by assuming an erect and stable posture and tuning in. The mantra for this meditation is Raa Maa Daa Saa, Saa Say So Hung, the same mantra used in the meditation for compassion and healing. Use the musical version of this mantra, recorded by Gurnam Singh, which is available from Ancient Healing Ways (see Resources, pg 87). For this meditation, your left hand will be placed, palm inward, on your navel point, connecting to your physical center and personal strength. The right hand will begin next to your right shoulder, palm facing forward, as if taking a pledge. Take a moderately deep breath and chant the mantra as your right hand comes forward so that it winds up fully extended parallel to the ground with the palm facing down. Then inhale again as you return to the

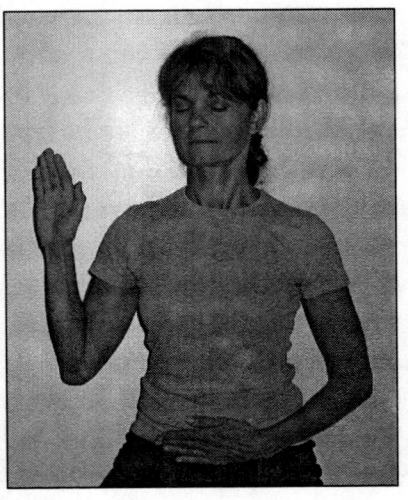

starting position and repeat. Each inhale plus the repetition of the mantra will take about ten seconds.

As you do the meditation, consciously send your blessings to whomever you wish. Start with eleven minutes and gradually work up to thirty-one minutes or even two and a half hours.

◎

The "God and Me" Meditation

The ultimate practice is the simplest. It is to constantly remember God, and call on that Infinite Presence-in-all. All the mantras given in this book are "names" of that Oneness and any mantra, from any tradition, can be used with each and every breath, to remind yourself of your divine nature.

As you go about your day, engaged in any activity, take your meditation practice with you. We practice meditation in the early morning hours, but meditation is how we live. With each breath, repeat your favorite mantra. You will forget, of course, and find yourself caught up in other thoughts. But each time you remember, bring yourself back to that one thought, the mantra.

Over time, you will see how it is possible to repeat God's name even while speaking or thinking about an important task. And, over time, more than anything else you might do, this practice will transform you and your life, and in turn give you the power to heal others with your presence. It is what a master does.

◎

Afterward

Persistent effort has led you to a place of no-effort and possible awakening. I have suggested a purposeless practice, free of striving. The intent has been to break attachment to self-improvement and illusory beliefs. Only within such a consciousness can anything truly original take place but you cannot predict what new truths you might discover, or when you will, or even if; nor can you plan what new or old paths you might be inspired to follow. This uncertainty is not an unfortunate part of the process; it is the essence of the process and part of its joy.

Be *un*-certain, maintaining the sense of flow and perhaps an expectancy of merger, but not insisting on knowing how it will all turn out. No good comes from trying to control the outcome of practice. Practice consistently and you will arrive at a place of mastery and a sense of your oneness with God. Let your only effort be to effortlessly practice with patience and persistence. A lifetime of desire has led you to this point of no desire and the joy of being.

This simple being-ness is not for you alone. Consider this: all you have done is so you might be better able to serve. Your clarity of consciousness, your compassion, all the other qualities you are developing are so you can uplift others and help to heal the world. If there is a goal in all this, let it be to develop your capacity for kindness, for knowing the most healing thing to do, for having the courage to do it. Let your mission be to reduce the suffering in the world. Give of yourself, not out of guilt or desire but as a clear expression of your super-conscious mind.

A sub text in all these lessons has been the need to transcend the desire for certainty and begin to allow ambiguity. This won't happen if you rely too heavily on outside authorities, including this one. We all want easy answers. We want the doctor to give an exact diagnosis and perfect, swift treatment. We may easily become attached to a "spiritual" authority and his or her prescriptions. It would be better to use these lessons to become unafraid of a little confusion and comfortable with a little pain. Set aside the need for fixed answers and notions of right and wrong. Practice with a completely open awareness, allowing whatever might appear. On this foundation you can build a mind empty of itself, a consciousness free of ego, judgment, and the need for authorities and dogma; a mind capable of surrender, gratitude, devotion, and compassion: a mind which knows what it is now, unconcerned with what it ought to become.

Use these lessons in a conscious and deliberate way. Select from among them whichever practices most serve your needs on any given day, or at any particular time in your life. But don't do any of this in an attempt at self-improvement. You are already a perfect soul and our purpose has been to help you to realize that. All you need do is to navigate skillfully through the fog of illusion. Eventually truth will shine though.

This is just the beginning.

Resources

If you have questions about any of the material in this book or would like further guidance in your meditation practice you can contact the author at Subaghk@gmail.com.

To purchase additional copies of this book, or for a free download of the book contact the author directly via email. The book can also be ordered from Spirit Voyage at www.Spiritvoyage.com or 888-735-4800.

For access to this and the author's other books you can also go to Amazon.com or BN.com and search for Subagh Khalsa.

To access teachers of Kundalini Yoga and Meditation (as taught by Yogi Bhajan) go to 3HO.org and click on the Yoga Teachers Directory.

To purchase recorded musical versions of some of the mantras used in this book (as well as many other products inspired by the teachings of Yogi Bhajan) go to Ancient Healing Ways at a-healing.com or at 1-800-359-2940. Similar materials are also available from Spirit Voyage at www.Spiritvoyage.com or 888-735-4800.

CPSIA information can be obtained at www.ICGtesting.com
233441LV00001B/72/P